WOMEN WORKERS

WOMEN WORKERS

M.I. SIDDIQUI

ANAMIKA PUBLISHERS & DISTRIBUTORS (P) LTD.
4697/3, 21A, Ansari Road, Daryaganj
New Delhi 110002
Phone: 23281655

First Published 2004

ISBN 81-7975-071-X

PRINTED IN INDIA

Published by Anamika Publishers & Distributors (P) Ltd., 4697/3, 21A, Ansari Road, Daryaganj, New Delhi 110002. Typeset by VGA, MU-61D, Pitampura, Delhi 110088 and Printed at Nagri Printers, Delhi.

Contents

Preface

Women have long been discriminated against in male dominated world, though almost equal in number Traditionally they were assigned the role of home-maker relegating them to a secondary position in the society. Women's reproductive role was enough to keep them away from earning for the self and family. Men being, the bread-earner hold top place in the world.

It took the world a long time to move towards gender equality. UN resolutions, ILO conventions and, NGOs interventions have improved the situation of women but equality especially at work is still a distant reality. Third world lags behind in the matter of women's equality in general and at work in particular.

Labour markets are segregated and women find place in the secondary segment where advancement opportunities are negligible. Statistics show women outnumber men only in occupations with low remuneration and poor working conditions. The dual responsibility of women hampers their career development and have attributes like late-entry, break and, immobility in terms of time, energy and space. Women's employment needs more attention at national and international levels.

The present work has a focus on working women at large. It also includes a case study which is a detailed analysis of women at work in a least developed country. It throws light on the region where women are at the centre of economic activity and also adds a new chapter to women studies.

The book has two parts. First part deals with the status of women across the globe and then leads to employment of women in various regions of the World. Second part is consisted of the case study which presents a detailed account of working women in Eritrea. The latter was completed during the stay in that country while working there for the Ministry of Labour and Human Welfare. However the first part has been written in India so as to complete the book. The endeavour has been to give a sketch of working women in various regions of the world.

It is hoped that those working in the field of women study would find it a useful contribution.

27th January 2003
Bareilly

M.I. Siddiqui

Acknowledgement

The author is thankful to all his teachers in the department of Economics, AMU, Aligarh particularly Mr. Abdul Mannan Siddiqui, who shaped the career and guided at every stage. All the colleagues there especially Prof. Ashok Mittal, Dr. S. Noman Ahmad, Dr. S.A. Rizvi and Saeed Khan deserve special mention.

Few colleagues at MJP Rohilkhand University like Prof. Yadav and Prof. Sinha and Honorary Librarian are acknowledged. The former for his love and affection and the latter for his friendship and his nagging to complete the book without further delay. Library staff is also acknowledged for providing material with a smiling face.

Eritrean colleagues namely Ato Tesfai, Berhane Alem, Hobtam and Abraham Negusse are thanked for their moral support and assistance whenever required.

Students play an important role in the life of every teacher and hence they deserve mention. Israr, Hurresh, Ashwini are particularly acknowledged here.

Abha, Samir and Amber are perennial source of inspiration without them no work could have been accomplished. Their unflinching support and encouragement is thankfully acknowledged.

Thanks are also due to Mr. Manoj Pandey for rendering secretarial assistance and Lal Bahadur for general assistance and help.

Part One

1

Status of Women

Introduction

Historically, traditionally and culturally women have not faired well at least in the matter of education and employment in any region of the world vis-à-vis men. Triple Es (Education, Employment and Empowerment) have boosted women's movement and taken as indicator of their freedom. Its testimony are all those conventions, seminars and conferences organized by international bodies like UN, and its various agencies, ILO and other organizations such as NGOs—national and international for the advancement of women all over the world. Statistics pertaining to female education reveal discrimination against women still persisting in developing countries, despite the fact that returns to women's education are high enough to match with that of men. The enrolment sex-ratio speaks about female children's plight, particularly in Asia. Whatever reasons are given female lag behind male children at primary, secondary and tertiary levels of education. If one has to forego education of any of one's children axe falls on girl child. It is mainly due to patriarchal society where male children are valued more than girls on account of lineage. India and China have, though poles apart socially and politically, preferential societal attitude towards male children. Consequently deliberate intervention in sex selection at birth has been increasingly practised not only in traditional but also in semi-modernised societies. Such attitude has its ramification in education, health and nutrition of female children.

Currently one of the most talked about and discussed subject has been women empowerment. It took centuries and a lot of deliberations to come to a stage where empowerment of women is on high agenda. Traditionally women were denied land title right to heir ancesteral property and even right to vote for a long time. Religion also blocked their way even in religious matters and hierarchy. Still there are monasteries, mosques and temples/deities where women are forbidden. Moreover religious scriptures of various faiths have assigned secondary status to women.

Women empowerment may not be possible unless equal legal rights are conferred upon them and accepted by the society. The importance of educating women has realized contribution of women without which economic development can not reach to its maximum. Still a lot is to be done in the area of accounting so a due place is given to women. Indirect contribution of women needs more attention than what the world has given to it. The equivalence accounting system is yet to be evolved and matured so that women's non-monetary work and time-use are recognized in terms of productivity, value-addition and reflected in a country's GNP.

Gender differential in employment and thereby in earnings is widespread. Key to economic prosperity is women's gainful employment. Moreover, status of women won't change to desirable extent unless financial or economic freedom is not attained by them.

Employment and earning enhancement is necessary to bring women at par with men. At present women's position in wage employment, self-employment and as employers is far from satisfactory. Whatever employment avenues are open to women especially in developing countries, these are low paid and least promotional. Wage differentials are significant and discriminating against women. They suffer from equal work but unequal wages' syndrome. Women are now favoured in employment as receptionist, school teachers, clerks and other low-paid jobs, thus, perpetuating their secondary status in the society and economy.

All it necessitates discussion on the status of women across the globe.

Women Across the Globe

The world habitats almost equal number of women, though the ratio of women to men has declined particularly during a quarter century from 1970 to 1995. The scenario which has changed in the last quarter of the century may largely be attributed to the regions of Asia, Africa and Latin America. These regions have experienced changed perspective on female children which in fact disturbed the sex-ratio. There has been deliberate intervention in sex selection due to societal attitude in general and customs or tradition in particular. Factors responsible for societal attitude are many but probably the most important has been patriarchy in most of societies. Still men-headed households outnumber women-headed households in developing countries where most of the population reside.

The sex ratio of population differs from region to region and

TABLE 1.1: Ratio of Women in the World

Region	Number of women per 100 men		% of world population
	1970	1995	
Developed Regions			21.6
Europe	106	105	
Other	101	103	
Africa			13.0
Northern Africa	99	97	
Sub-Saharan Africa	104	102	
Latin America & Caribbean			8.4
Latin America	99	100	
Caribbean	106	103	
Asia and Pacific			57.0
Eastern Asia	98	97	
S. Eastern Asia	99	100	
Southern Asia	95	95	
Central Asia	–	104	
Western Asia	90	92	
Oceania	93	95	
World	99.6	98.6	

Sources: (i) UN, Demographic Yearbook, various issues,
(ii) UN, The Sex and Age Distribution of the World Populations, E 93, XIII. 3

no claim can be made about any particular pattern in specific regions. Developed region has, for example, higher ratio of women per hundred men. So is the case with sub-Saharan Africa and Caribbean. Hence such inferences that developed regions have higher women to men ratio than developing regions do not match facts and figures. However, northern Africa, Asia and Pacific have low ratio of women to men. Indiscriminate intervention in sex selection in a pre-natal stage has largely caused a lower women to men ratio, particularly in Asian countries including India.

However, encouraging factor is that women now outnumber men across the globe. It may, therefore, be expected that a kind of stability in sex ratio, particularly in the old age group would be experienced in countries around the world. A declining mortality rate which has been higher for female children is one of the reason to 'stabilize' or even enhance sex ratio in favour of women.

The myth if any, is broken that developed regions have sex ratio

TABLE 1.2: Percentage of Women-Headed Households in the World

(Based on 1990 Census round)

Region	Percentage
Developed Region	24
Africa:	
Northern Africa	13
Sub-Saharan Africa	20
Latin America and Caribbean	
Latin America	21
Caribbean	35
Asia and Pacific	
Eastern Asia	27
South Eastern Asia	18
Southern Asia[a]	13
Western Asia[b]	12
Oceania	17

[a]Hongkong and Republic of Korea
[b]Israel and Kuwait
Source: UN, Women's Indicators and Statistics Database, E. 95 XVII. 6

in favour of women as the same may be seen from the Table for sub-Saharan Africa and Caribbean. Moreover, the situation should be analyzed keeping in view the regional distribution of world's population. Women-headed household percentages will make further clarification regarding their status in different societies.

The highest percentage of women-headed households has been recorded in the Caribbean region followed by developed region. It again speaks about the status of women in different parts of the world where qualitative difference does not favour women irrespective of either the level of development or backwardness.

Women's percentage distribution in urban and rural segments needs consideration since it may be taken as prelude to employment and work opportunities.

TABLE 1.3: Population Distribution and Women/hundred Men, 1995

Country	Total population	Urban per cent	Women/hundred men	
			Urban	Rural
Developed Region				
Albania	3,390	37	85	101
Australia	18,338	85	102	90
Austria	7,861	61	112	101
Belarus[a]	10,152	65	112	118
Bulgaria	8,887	71	104	104
Canada	25,837	78	106	94
Croatia[b]	4,784	54	109	104
Czech Rep.[c]	10,330	75	107	103
Czechoslovakia (former)	15,876	81	106	101
Denmark	5,192	85	105	88
Estonia	1,571	73	114	106
Finland	5,046	60	110	99
France	57,769	73	107	100
Germany	81,264	86	107	98
Greece	10,253	65	105	100
Hungary	10,471	68	110	105
Iceland	268	92	100	83
Ireland	3,469	58	106	92
Japan	1,25,879	78	102	106

(*Contd.*)

Country	Total population	Urban per cent	Women/hundred men	
			Urban	Rural
Latvia	2,650	73	115	109
Lithuania	3,771	72	111	109
Luxembourg	386	86	104	100
Malta	367	89	103	100
Netherlands	15,499	89	102	98
Newzealand	3,552	84	105	89
Norway	4,357	77	105	93
Poland	38,736	64	108	100
Portugal	9,884	36	112	104
Moldova[a] Rep.	4,335	47	108	112
Romania	23,505	56	102	104
Russian Fed.[a]	1,47,022	73	114	113
Slovenia[c]	1,990	51	109	103
Spain	39,276	81	105	96
Sweden	8,773	85	104	89
Switzerland	6,955	64	108	97
Ukraine[a]	51,452	67	115	121
U.K.	58,093	89	105	98
U.S.	2,63,138	76	107	98
Yugoslavia (ex)	24,113	61	104	99
Africa				
Algeria	28,581	56	100	99
Benin	5,399	42	100	104
Botswana	1,433	31	92	116
Burkina Faso	10,352	20	89	105
Burundi	6,343	6	79	106
Cameroon	13,275	45	95	107
C. African Rep.	3,429	51	106	106
Chad	6,361	37	90	110
Comoros	653	31	97	97
Congo	2,590	43	95	112
Cote d' Ivoire	14,401	44	91	102
Egypt	58,519	45	95	98
Equ. Guinea	400	31	97	106
Eritrea	2,622	15	117	98
Ethiopia	58,039	13	114	99
Gabon	1,367	50	89	118
Gambia	980	26	103	102

(*Contd.*)

Country	Total population	Urban per cent	Women/hundred men	
			Urban	Rural
Ghana	17,453	36	103	100
Guinea	6,700	30	93	101
Kenya	27,885	28	83	107
Lesotho	1,977	23	119	101
Liberia	3,039	51	90	107
Libyan A.J.	5407	86	91	95
Madagascar	14,155	27	103	101
Malawi	11,304	14	84	106
Mali	10,797	27	100	105
Mauritania	2,335	54	91	116
Mauritius	1,130	41	103	100
Morocco	28,260	48	99	101
Mozambique	16,359	34	91	109
Namibia	1,688	31	85	106
Niger	9,102	23	100	102
Nigeria	1,26,929	39	95	106
Rwanda	8,330	6	80	104
Senegal	8,387	42	100	100
S. Africa	42,741	51	98	105
Sudan	28,960	25	92	101
Swaziland	859	31	85	112
Togo	4,138	31	100	103
Tunisia	8,933	59	98	98
Uganda	20,405	13	102	101
Tanzania	30,742	24	92	106
Zaire	43,814	29	97	104
Zambia	9,381	43	94	108
Zimbabwe	11,536	32	85	110
Latin America				
Argentina	34,264	87	105	85
Barbados	261	48	112	104
Bolivia	8,074	54	104	99
Brazil	1,61,382	79	103	91
Chile	14,237	86	106	83
Colombia	35,101	73	108	87
Costa Rica	3,424	50	108	89
Cuba	11,091	76	104	87
Dominican Rep.	7,915	65	103	86

(Contd.)

Country	Total population	Urban per cent	Women/hundred men	
			Urban	Rural
Ecuador	11,822	61	103	93
El Salvador	5,768	47	114	97
Guatemala	10,621	41	104	94
Guyana	834	35	109	98
Haiti	7,180	32	125	95
Honduras	5,968	48	106	92
Jamaica	2,547	55	107	93
Mexico	93,670	75	103	94
Nicaragua	4,433	63	113	92
Panama	2,659	55	105	88
Paraguay	4,893	51	104	91
Peru	23,854	72	99	98
Puerto Rico	3,691	77	108	97
Trinidad Tabogo	1,305	67	107	94
Uruguay	3,186	90	110	71
Venezuela	21,483	93	100	86
Asia and Pacific				
Afghanistan	23,196	20	93	96
Armenia	3,305	67	106	100
Azerbaijan	7,021	54	104	107
Bahrain	578	84	72	88
Bangladesh	1,28,251	20	79	99
Brunei Dar.	288	58	95	94
Combodia	9,447	13	104	109
China	12,38,319	30	93	95
Cyprus	736	56	100	100
East Timor	835	15	85	99
Georgia	5,401	55	114	107
Hongkong	5,932	95	94	88
India	9,31,044	27	88	96
Indonesia	2,01,477	33	100	101
Iran	66,720	60	96	98
Iraq	21,224	75	95	102
Israel	5,884	93	103	94
Jordan	4,755	71	95	96
Kazakhstan	16,964	57	110	102
Korea, Rep.	45,182	78	98	98
Kuwait	1,604	97	130	43

(*Contd.*)

Country	Total population	Urban per cent	Women/hundred men	
			Urban	Rural
Kyrgyzstan	4,258	38	111	101
Lao, PDR	4,882	22	103	103
Lebanon	3,028	87	105	105
Malaysia	20,125	47	98	99
Maldives	248	33	77	99
Myanmar	46,548	26	100	101
Nepal	22,124	14	87	96
Pakistan	1,34,974	35	88	95
Philippines	69,257	46	99	96
Sri Lanka	18,346	22	96	102
Syria	14,775	52	96	101
Tajikistan	5,092	32	104	100
Thailand	58,265	25	106	100
Turkey	62,032	69	92	105
Turkmenistan	3,523	45	103	103
U.A.E.	1,785	84	50	58
Uzbekistan	19,810	41	104	101
Vietnam	73,811	21	102	103
Yemen	13,897	34	89	110
Oceania				
American Samoa	55	49	97	94
Cook Islands	17	26	93	91
Fiji	762	41	10	95
French Polynesia	222	67	96	87
Guam	146	59	83	91
Kiribati	79	39	102	102
Marshall Islands	55	67	97	92
Micronesia	122	55	96	98
New Caledonia	180	62	97	94
N. Mariana Islands	48	28	107	84
Palau	17	60	86	85
Papua New Guinea	4,344	18	60	92
Samoa	159	23	91	88
Solomon Islands	378	17	76	94
Tonga	99	41	102	97
Vanuatu	169	19	89	95

Source: U.N. World Urbanization Prospects: The 1992 Rev. E 93, XIII.
Note: Reference year differs.

The availability of women with respect to men may be summed up as shown below.

TABLE 1.4: Urban Women ≥ 100 per Hundred Men Across the Globe

Region	Countries
Developed	All countries except Albania
Africa	Algeria, Benin, C. African Rep., Eritrea, Ethiopia, Gambia, Ghana, Lesotho, Madagascar, Mali, Mauritius, Niger, Senegal, Togo, Uganda
Latin America	All countries except Peru
Asia and Pacific	Armenia, Azerbaijan, Combodia, Cyprus, Georgia, Indonesia, Israel, Kazakhstan, Kuwait, Kyrgyzstan, Lao, Lebanan, Myanmar, Tajikistan, Thailand, Turkmenistan, Uzbekistan, Vietnam
Oceania	Fiji, Kiribati, Tonga

Source: Compiled from U.N., *op. cit.*

Similarly countries where urban and or rural women's number is less than per hundred men may be pointed out.

Imbalances in sex ratio in urban area are more in the regions of Africa, Asia and Pacific, and Oceania. Similarly women to men ratio in rural area show inequality in developed region, Latin America and Caribbean, Asia and Pacific, and Oceania. In fact Oceania has imbalances in both urban and rural area. Table 1.5 brings out contrast between developed and developing regions in the matter of women's number per hundred of men. Africa has deficient number of women in its urban areas, while developed region and, Latin America and Caribbean have less women per one hundred men in rural area. But Asia and Pacific, and Oceania present a different picture where largely less number of women is found for men in urban and rural area both. There position of women is different in terms of availability and in contrast to developed and Latin American regions.

Women's Education and Returns

Status of women in terms of primary-secondary enrolment has not been better even in developed region. This situation is more worse

TABLE 1.5: Countries with less than 100 women per 100 men—Urban and Rural

Regions	Countries	
	Urban	Rural
Developed	Albania	Australia, Canada, Denmark, Finland, Germany, Iceland, Ireland, Netherlands, Newzealand, Norway, Poland, Spain, Sweden, Switzerland, UK, US, Yugoslavia (Former), USSR (Former)
Africa	Botswana, Burkina-faso, Burundi, Cameroon, Chad, Comoros, Congo, Cote d' Ivoire, Egypt, Equi. Guinea, Gabon, Guinea, Kenya, Liberia, Libya, Malawi, Mauritania, Morocco, Mozambique, Namibia, Nigeria, Rwanda, S. Africa, Sudan, Swaziland, Tunisia, Tanzania, Zaire, Zambia, Zimbabwe	Algeria, Comoros, Egypt, Eritrea, Ethiopia, Libya, Tunisia
Latin America and Caribbean	Peru	Argentina, Bolivia, Brazil, Chile, Cambodia, Costa Rica, Cuba, Dominican, Rep., Ecuador, El Salvador, Guatemala, Guyana, Hati, Honduras, Jamaica, Mexico, Nicaragua, Panama, Paraguay, Peru, Puerto Rico, Trinidad & Tobago, Uruguay, Venezuela
Asia and Pacific	Afghanistan, Bahrain, Bangladesh, Brunei, China, E. Timor, Hongkong, India, Iran, Iraq, Jordon, Korea Rep. Malaysia, Maldives, Nepal, Pakistan, Philippines, Sri Lanka, Syria, Turkey, UAE, Yemen	Afghanistan, Bahrain, Bangladesh, Brunei, China, E. Timor, Hongkong, India, Iran, Israel Jordon, Korea Rep., Kuwait, Malaysia, Maldives, Nepal, Pakistan, Philippines, UAE
Oceania	American Samoa, Cook Islands, French Polynesia, Guam, Marshall Islands, New Caledonia, Micronesia, Palau, Papua New Guinea, Samoa, Solomon Islands, Vanuatu	American Samoa, Cook Islands, Fiji, French Polynesia, Guam, Kiribati, Marshall Islands, New Caledonia, N. Mariana Islands, Micronesia, Palau, Papua New Guinea, Samoa, Solomon, Islands, Tonga, Vanuatu

TABLE 1.6: Comparative Situation of Women Gross Enrolment at Primary-Secondary levels, 1990

Region	Countries where women Gross Enrolment Ratio is higher than men
Developed	Australia, Austria, Denmark, Estonia, Finland, France, Hungary, Ireland, Italy, Japan, Latvia, Lithuania, Luxembourg, Newzealand, Norway, Poland, Romania, Spain, Sweden, UK, USSR (Former)
Africa	Botswana, Lesotho, Namibia, South Africa
Latin America and Caribbean	Argentina, Bahamas, Chile, Colombia, Cuba, Dominican Rep., El Salvador, Guyana, Honduras, Jamaica, Nicaragua, Panama, Surinam, Trinidad & Tobago, Venezuela
Asia and Pacific	Cyprus, Hongkong, Israel, Jordon, Mangolia, Qatar, Sri Lanka
Oceania	Nil

off in developing countries, since there are fewer countries in Africa, Asia and Pacific where women have higher ratio in terms of primary-secondary level enrolment.

Table 1.6 shows that the number of countries in Africa, Asia and Pacific is very small where female gross enrolment ratio is higher than men. This situation does not improve for the gross enrolment at third level of education. Even in developed region the number of such countries where gross enrolment of women per 100,000 population exceeds than that of men is very small. Only Albania, Australia, Bulgaria, Canada, Denmark, Finland, France, Iceland, Norway, Poland, Portugal, Sweden and the U.K. have larger number of females vis-à-vis men at the third level of education. In Africa only three countries namely, Lesotho, Namibia and South Africa may claim higher enrolment of women at tertiary level of education. Latin America and Caribbean region has seven countries *viz.* Argentina, Barbados, Colombia, Cuba, Panama, Surinam and Uruguay have higher women enrolment than men at this level. Asia and pacific region has Bahrain, Brunei Daressalam, Cyprus, Kuwait, the Philippines, Qatar, Thailand and, the UAE where number of women per 1,00,000 population surpasses men enrolment at the third level of education. Oceania has no country which may fall in this category.

Therefore women are not better placed than men in the matter of education either in developed or developing region despite efforts made at national, regional and international levels. However, situation has improved over the past decades and it calls for concerted efforts in this direction. "The educational miracle did not extend enough to women...." (Tilak, 1994).

Education has its impact on development as investment in education does bring returns to the individual and nation both. It is equally true for female education which sometimes is mistakenly taken as 'consumption' or at the most welfare expenditure particularly in developing countries (King & Hill, 1992). There is, however, no society where female education is not crucial for development.

Returns to education, male and female both, have been proved beyond doubt and measured for number of countries (Psacharopolos, 1973). Mincer's discrimination index measures gender bias to the returns to male and female and commonly used estimate may be given as:

$$\sum_{t=s}^{n} \left[\frac{(E_t - C_t)}{(p + r^*)}\right] = 0$$

where E_t, C_t and *s-n* represent earning differentials of a given level of education over time in years, cost of education and working life of an individual.

Mincerian method or earning function takes the following regression form:

$$\text{In } Y = \alpha + \beta_1 S + \beta_2 E + \beta_3 EX^2 + \epsilon$$

where Y, S, Ex represent annual earnings, years of schoolings, labour market experience while α, β_i are intercept and regression coefficients.

Some interesting results have been obtained on the basis of returns to education by gender in Asian countries where returns are either equal or higher for women than men (Tilak, 1994, p. 91). It is also argued that rates of return to women's non-market contribution is taken into consideration (Woodhall, 1973).

Therefore, a strong case is there to invest in women's education in developing countries.

Time-Use

The dual role of women as worker and home maker distinguishes females from males. These are not only biological differences but also social responsibilities which make women different from men. Women do productive activities along with reproductive function while men do not perform the latter in the same way. Reproductive role of women has in fact made them responsible for child bearing to rearing and it ties women to home. Traditional and oriental societies have strong perception of women as home makers and assign them household chores and childcare exclusive but unpaid work. The scenario has considerably changed in Western society and narrowed the gap between total work hours of men and women. The same may not be claimed in respect of developing countries.

Time-use may be categorized into : (i) paid work (ii) unpaid work (iii) household chores and, (iv) child care. As a result of time-use survey conducted in various countries produced the following time-use allocation by men and women (Rao & Latha, 1998, Vol. 1, pp. 286-87).

Figure 1.1 brings out gap between total and paid work hours of women per week and thus shows long but unpaid work hours

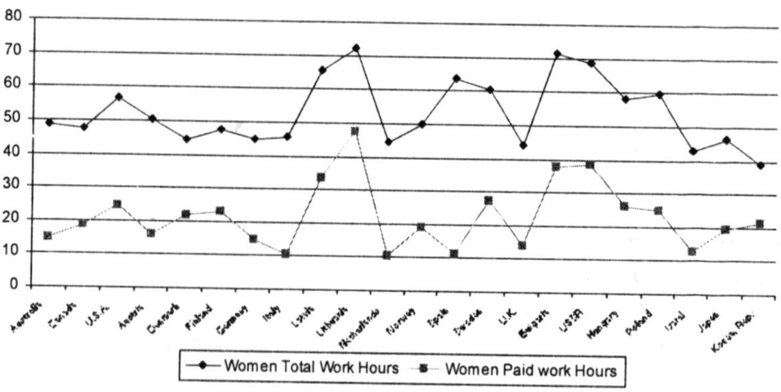

Figure 1.1

TABLE 1.7: Time-use of Women and Men (Work hrs./Week)

Country	Ref. year	Total		Paid work		Unpaid		H.H. chores		Child care		Personal care and free time	
		W	M	W	M	W	M	W	M	W	M	W	M
N. America and Australia													
Australia	1992	48.7	48.9	14.7	31.4	34.0	17.5	28.2	15.9	5.7	1.6	115.6	115.9
Canada	1992	47.6	47.1	18.7	31.5	28.9	15.6	24.7	13.9	4.2	1.8	116.8	116.3
USA	1986	56.4	59.5	24.5	41.3	31.9	18.1	29.9	17.4	2.0	0.8	112.0	109.0
W. Europe													
Austria	1992	50.2	46.0	15.9	32.7	34.3	13.3	30.5	12.0	3.9	1.3	112.9	116.3
Denmark	1987	44.3	46.2	21.8	35.0	22.5	11.2	20.7	10.5	1.9	0.7	119.6	117.5
Finland	1987	47.5	44.3	23.1	31.7	24.4	12.6	20.9	11.4	3.5	1.2	115.3	119.2
Germany F. Rep.	1991/92	44.7	41.8	14.7	29.5	30.0	12.3	26.8	11.0	3.2	1.3	119.7	122.2
Italy	1988/89	45.5	36.2	10.6	27.9	32.8	7.6	2.1	0.7	34.9	8.3	115.4	123.9
Latvia	1987	65.7	60.2	33.4	43.8	32.3	16.4	25.1	13.2	7.2	3.2	101.5	106.6
Lithuania	1988	72.2	66.6	47.5	50.6	24.7	16.0	21.7	14.3	3.0	1.7	94.4	99.8
Netherlands	1988	44.6	44.5	10.4	26.6	34.2	17.9	30.6	16.5	3.6	1.4	118.3	117.7
Norway	1990	49.8	49.1	19.3	30.8	30.6	18.3	25.3	16.2	5.3	2.1	114.5	115.6
Spain	1991	63.8	40.6	11.4	29.4	52.4	11.2	35.8	8.6	16.7	2.6	101.2	123.2
Sweden	1990/91	60.5	61.2	27.3	41.1	33.2	20.2	28.0	18.1	5.2	2.1	105.0	104.6
UK	1984	44.1	38.2	14.1	26.8	30.0	11.4	26.4	10.3	3.6	1.1	124.0	130.0

(*Contd.*)

Country	Ref. year	Total		Paid work		Unpaid		H.H. chores		Child care		Personal care and free time	
		W	M	W	M	W	M	W	M	W	M	W	M
E. Europe and former USSR													
Bulgaria	1988	71.3	62.3	37.7	46.9	33.7	15.3	29.3	14.3	4.3	1.1	97.0	106.0
Former USSR	1986	68.6	65.1	38.5	49.0	30.1	16.1	25.7	14.6	4.4	1.5	99.0	103.0
Hungary	1986	58.2	53.2	26.0	41.1	32.2	12.1	27.8	10.5	4.4	1.6	107.3	111.9
Poland	1984	59.8	51.9	24.9	42.2	34.9	9.7	30.5	7.7	4.4	2.0	106.8	114.8
Asia													
Israel	1991/92	42.8	42.7	12.8	32.7	30.0	10.0	22.8	7.6	7.2	2.5	118.0	116.9
Japan	1991	46.6	43.6	19.5	40.8	27.1	2.8	24.5	2.5	2.6	0.4	118.0	120.2
Korea, Rep.	1990	39.0	37.5	21.4	35.4	17.6	2.1	17.2	2.0	0.5	0.1	129.0	130.6

which are significantly higher than work hours of men. A graphical depiction of household chores and child care work hours may show the difference between men and women.

Child care and household are supposed to be exclusive women area of work at least in developing countries. Even in developed region where perception of responsibilities has changed and men share some of the responsibilities in these matters difference between time hours of women and men are significant and visible.

Panel A of the Figure 1.2 shows striking difference in time use of women and men for household chores. Women have to spend much more time on household chores than men not only in Asian countries but developed region as well. It turns out a universal phenomenon that women shoulder the responsibility of home maker and taking care of children more than men. The shade of degree may be different between developed and developing countries as the latter still have age-old traditions and customs. Hence women have a shade more traditional role in developing countries than what is there in developed region, except Japan and Korea which still preserve their traditional values.

Last but not the least, women have to give more hours for unpaid jobs as compared to men. It is again because of perception, religious values have not completely broken the chains of the so-called social responsibility of women despite universal movement

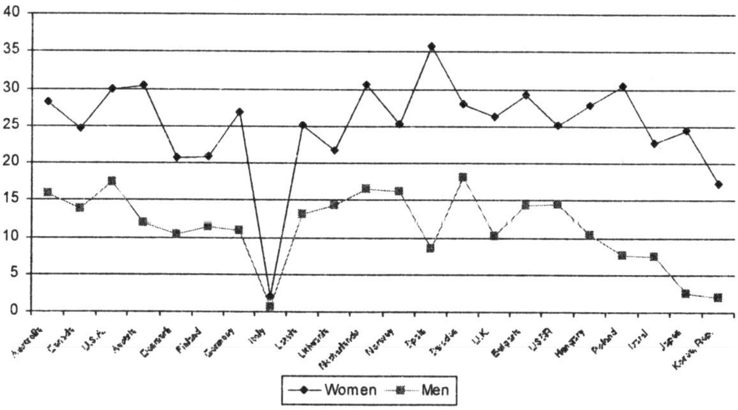

Figure 1.2: Household Chores hours/week

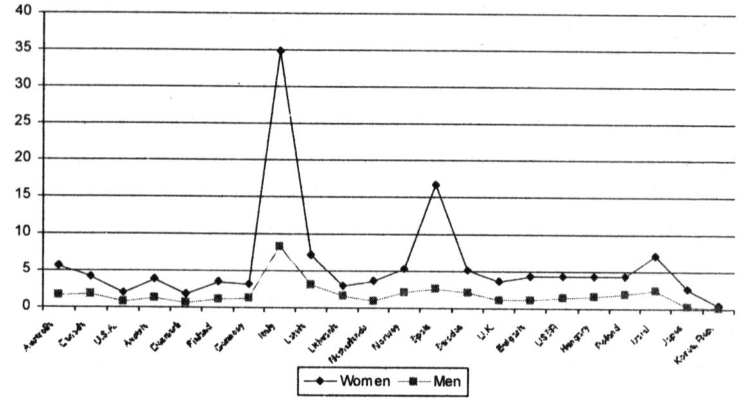

Figure 1.3

for women liberation. On this count i.e. less hours for paid work and more hours for unpaid work, *inter alia*, gender wage differentials appear. How far women work less for paid work in comparison of their counterparts in different regions of the world may be seen from Figure 1.4.

There is not a single country in any region where work hours of women are higher than men showing a gender bias towards men. Figure 1.3 shows discrepancy since men's working hour curve does

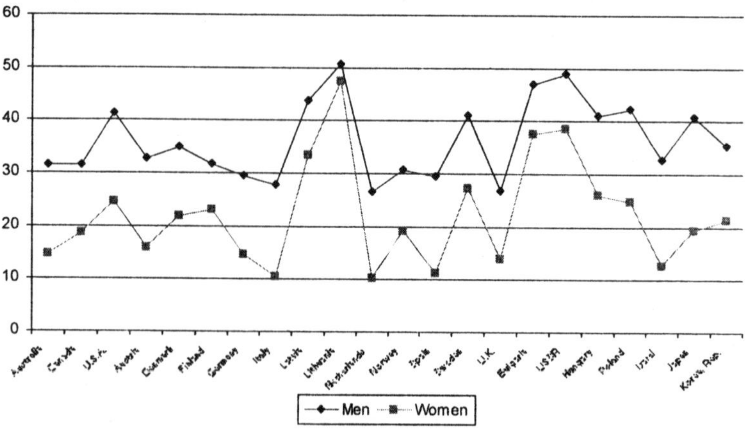

Figure 1.4

not intersects with the curve depicting working hours of women. Therefore women are discriminated against in case of paid work and naturally their earnings would be less than that of men, irrespective of the nature and development level of the society.

It may safely be deduced that, as evident from various figures, women have more unpaid hours, devote more time for household chores and child care and less work hours for paid work thus causing wage differential against them. And it appears as universal phenomenon, that is, common in developing and developed regions.

Sum-up

Education is one of the most important tool of women empowerment. However gender disparity in education of women has been reflected from their ratio at primary-secondary level. The situation is no more better at tertiary level of education. Though the societal attitude has been changing regarding female education, however, desired level is still to be achieved in this direction.

Returns to women's education is higher as difference has been high enough to fill the gap. It, therefore, makes a strong case for women's education.

Time-use of male and female shows that women spend more time on unpaid work. Similarly household chores and childcare are still considered responsibilities of women and men's share is negligible. Due to reproductive and productive roles women bear more social responsibilities and could not devote as much time as men do for paid work. Women are thus discriminated against and a lot is still to be done. Equal partners in life should be given equal employment opportunity and for the same work, same wages must be given to women as their right.

2

Employment of Women: An Overview

Gender inequality in general and discriminatory practices in particular led to proliferation of literature on issues pertaining to women. Employment has attracted enough attention to make a strong case for women as it results in economic empowerment. A gainful employment provides women not only financial freedom to a large extent but they also become a part in decision-making, a right which has long been denied to them particularly in developing regions. Simultaneously their status in the family gets elated.

Why women have no equality in employment and are discriminated against? Its reasons are many and a host of factors may be found to explain the phenomenon. In the world of work men's dominance has been there as legacy since they were, and still are, considered bread-winner for the family. This conception of men as bread-earners is still valid since widely believed, recognized and accepted in developing countries. Though the single family and working parents in the West and elsewhere have diluted the notion and acceptance of men as bread-winner but traditional or even semi-modernised societies in developing region could not dispense with the idea.

Societal attitude and structure for a long time perpetuated the thought that women have less potential and capability for work and biological factor makes them more suitable for family responsibilities in a natural way. They can not shirk away from their responsibility of child bearing and rearing as women are meant for it. Their social responsibilities were taken as a reason not to enter the arena of men, that is employment. It is no more prevalent in developed region but still significant in developing countries on social and religious grounds. The societal attitude has not changed enough to bring gender equality in employment.

There has been and still is, segmentation of women in employment. They are generally accepted and considered suitable for low paid jobs with very little promotional avenues, or for marginal economic activities. Women are consequently predominant in the occupations of clerks, receptionists, house keepers, primary teaching and nursing in most of the countries. In India, Pakistan, Bangladesh and West Asia women are largely in such occupations due to suitability factor. The labour market is still highly segmented for women across the globe. Even in the west equal work does not command equal pay.

Women as a whole have less access to education, training and skill development since they are largely considered as home makers. The sex ratio of children at primary and secondary levels is biased against females, if not in developed region then certainly in developing regions. At tertiary level the situation of women education is no better as they have significant presence in liberal arts and not in professional courses—which leads to not so high echelons of employment and earnings.

Another factor, which acts as deterrent to women employment has been their immobility in terms of time, energy and space. Due to their familial responsibilities women are not considered mobile in terms of space. Hence they are discriminated against, at least in developed countries. A married women in general and with children in particular is less mobile than a married man with children. Women of course have familial ties in developing world making them less mobile.

Legislative provisions are indeed inadequate in terms of implementation and hence women are discriminated against in employment. Sometimes legislative provision to protect women turn out harmful for them in the matter of employment. It needs a careful examination from the view point of discrimination.

The national accounting system, particularly regarding GNP of a country relies on monetary contribution called as economic accounting but over looks social accounting. It, thus undermines women's contribution of non-monetary work largely done by them and keeps them at the periphery of remunerative system. An equivalence system has not only to be devised but also made operative.

These are some of the factors responsible for gender inequality in employment. However theoretical framework of women employment may be discussed in terms of labour market theories.

Theoretical Framework: Dual Labour Market Theory

Employment of women generally finds explanation and justification in dual labour market theory. In case of female employment supply side has been given more attention than demand side while it is observed that when demand increases sharply, women's participation rate in labour force also jumps up. But in situations like this or otherwise labour market structure and the forces which draw female labour are not paid enough attention (Barron & Norris, 1974). Since labour market is generally segmented into a number of structures, it is necessary to differentiate the segments and structures. The labour market is generally divided into primary and secondary segments. Employment in the primary sector has well paid jobs with promotional avenues and better working conditions including higher security. On contrary, jobs in the secondary sector have low payment without or negligible promotion opportunities and less security of jobs. Primary sector employment with promotion opportunities exists due to highly structured internal labour market in the sense that jobs have the hierarchy based on skills. Moreover higher places in the hierarchy are largely filled through promotion from lower position when the higher level of skills has been attained. External labour market has a little role to play in the recruitment. While employment in the secondary segment is from external labour market and not through internal promotion. Simple reason is: secondary segment has no structured internal market. Employment in the secondary sector requires unskilled or semi-skilled workers and thus recruited from outside. Such jobs have no promotional avenues.

Another distinction between segment with structured internal labour market and unstructured labour market due to internal mobility in the former, i.e. primary sector is always vertical while it is horizontal in the secondary market which has no organization of hierarchy. The career opportunities in the primary sector are internally mobile that is, advancement in the organizational hierarchy. Whereas workers in the secondary sector which are unskilled or with very little skills move from occupations to occupations and one industry to another.

Primary labour market creates or have structure so as to retain highly skilled workers in the firm which reduces labour turnover. Therefore scarce skills are rewarded in terms of higher pay and good working conditions. Moreover it is in the interest of employers to buy off group of workers with scarce skills so they expand primary sector. But their interest also lies in maintaining low earnings and volatility in the secondary sector. It is because there is a large supply of labour at lower wages. In such a situation working conditions, job status, and job security would be poor for the reserve army of workers.

A high degree of segmentation of occupations exists for male and female workers where the latter are generally paid low wages. Women, therefore, belong to the secondary sector as its characteristic is poor earnings and low level of skills. Moreover, women possess those attributes which characterise secondary sector such as easily dispensible, differentiated by conventional social difference, poor inclination to acquire training etc., low on economism, less solidaristic relations with colleagues (Jha *et al.*, 1998, p. 82). All these attributes of women workers bring them into the folds of secondary sector of the labour market. Thus dual labour market theory explains the employment of female labour and occupational segmentation between male and female workers.

The dual labour market theory may not be taken as the theory of female labour market but it does provide an explanation for occupational segregation of women workers. And also to why women workers get less remunerative jobs with horizontal expansion due to lack of skill based organization of hierarchy.

Women in the Labour Force by Industrial Sector

Distribution of women in labour force is asymmetrical and accounts more in the secondary segment of the labour market characterized by low earning and poor working conditions. However situation of women's participation in the labour force varies from region to region.

It is interesting that women's economic activity rate, by and large, has gone up in almost all the regions. Whereas adult economic activity rate of men experienced a gradual decline over the period. It may be contrary to the expectations of those who portray a gloomy picture of women in the matter of employment and economic activities.

Adult economic activity rates worked out for men and women are given in Figures 2.1 to 2.4.

Figure 2.1 depicts a generally fallings percentage of men's economic activity rates over the period 1970 to 1990 in every region of the world. On the contrary, women economic rates, over the same period, has an increasing trend in almost all the regions. Therefore similar trends in economic activity rates have been found for men and women, though of a contrary nature.

However its not clear from the figure that how the labour is distributed between male and female workers. Table 2.1 shows percentage distribution of labour force by sex.

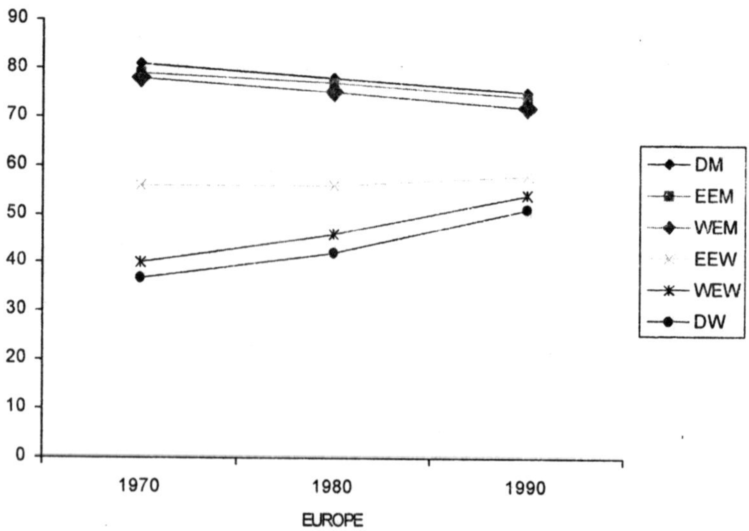

Figure 2.1

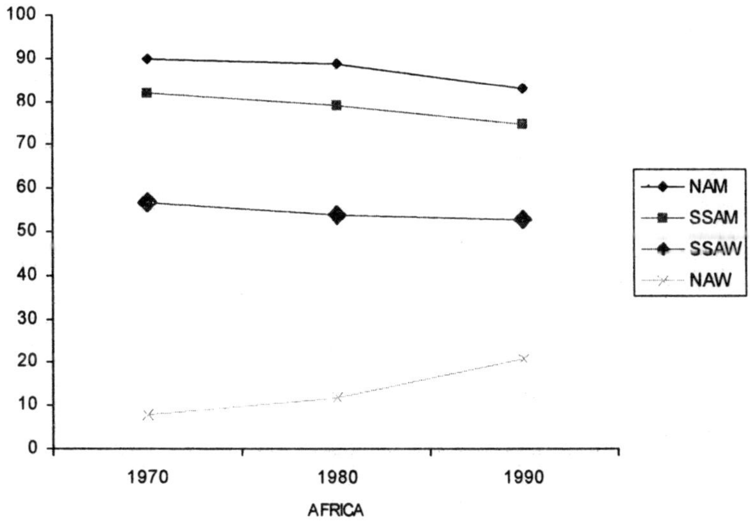

Figure 2.2

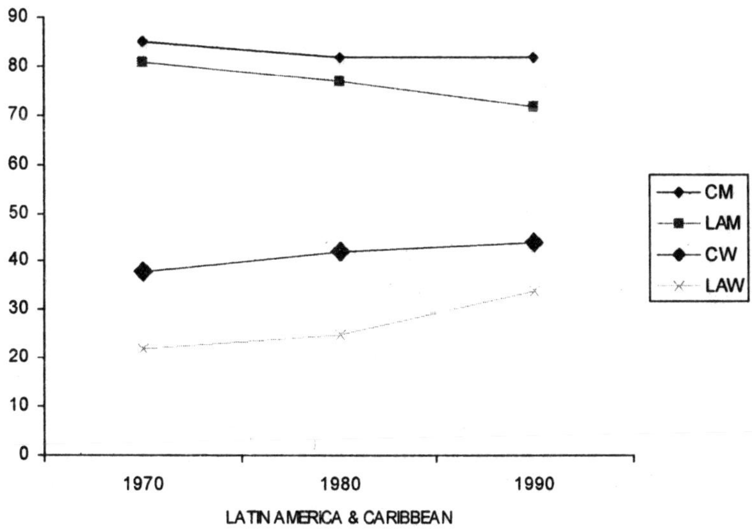

Figure 2.3

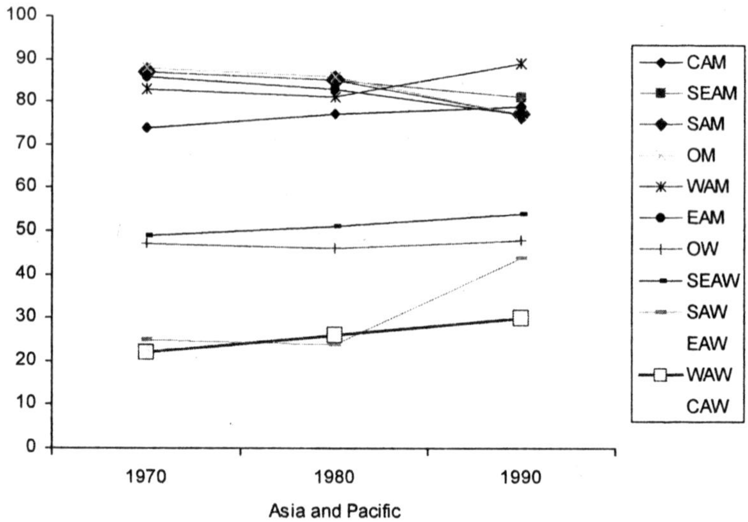

Figure 2.4

TABLE 2.1: Distribution of Labour Force by Sex, 1994

(Percentage)

Country	Agriculture		Industry		Services	
	Women	Men	Women	Men	Women	Men
Albania	57	48	20	29	2	3
Australia	6	6	13	38	81	56
Austria	3	3	23	50	74	47
Belarus	13	26	36	45	51	29
Bosnia-Herzegovina	11	5	39	56	50	39
Bulgaria	12	12	43	55	46	33
Canada	2	4	15	40	83	57
Croatia	13	15	29	38	58	46
Czech Rep.	9	13	37	54	55	33
Denmark	1	6	15	40	84	54
Estonia	11	18	34	49	55	33
Finland	4	4	20	47	76	48
France	3	4	20	46	77	49
Germany	6	5	33	54	60	40
Greece	27	16	19	36	53	48

(Contd.)

Country	Agriculture		Industry		Services	
	Women	Men	Women	Men	Women	Men
Hungary	10	19	32	43	58	39
Iceland	2	6	23	48	75	46
Ireland	2	14	20	44	78	42
Italy	6	4	26	43	68	53
Latvia	12	19	33	47	55	34
Lithuania	10	23	35	47	55	30
Luxembourg	4	2	9	37	87	60
Malta	4	3	15	49	81	47
Netherlands	2	5	8	32	90	62
Newzealand	9	12	18	36	73	51
Norway	5	6	8	35	87	59
Poland	27	27	25	45	48	28
Portugal	45	7	19	54	35	39
Moldova Rep.	25	37	27	34	48	29
Romania	17	18	46	55	37	27
Russian Fed.	9	17	35	48	56	34
Slovakia	8	14	40	38	51	48
Slovenia	4	3	40	53	56	94
Spain	6	9	17	43	77	48
Sweden	3	4	10	40	88	56
Switzerland	4	5	16	38	81	57
Macedonia	18	19	44	41	39	40
Ukraine	15	23	34	46	51	31
UK	1	3	15	42	84	55
USA	1	4	17	40	81	56
Yugoslavia	29	27	27	39	43	35
Africa						
Algeria	10	16	21	34	69	51
Angola	87	58	2	17	11	25
Benin	64	54	4	12	31	34
Botswana	78	41	3	31	19	27
Burkina Faso	85	85	4	6	11	9
Burundi	98	87	1	4	1	9
Cameroon	64	51	4	16	32	33
Cape Verde	14	50	31	30	54	21
C. African Rep.	63	60	5	12	31	28
Chad	80	75	2	7	19	18
Comoros	84	76	3	10	13	15
Congo	83	45	2	19	15	36

(Contd.)

Country	Agriculture		Industry		Services	
	Women	Men	Women	Men	Women	Men
Cote d'Ivoire	62	50	8	13	30	38
Djibouti	80	71	8	11	12	18
Egypt	8	42	20	25	71	33
Equ. Guinea	82	38	3	22	15	39
Eritrea	80	71	8	11	12	18
Ethiopia	80	71	8	11	12	18
Gabon	84	63	3	18	13	19
Gambia	91	74	3	12	6	14
Ghana	50	55	17	20	33	24
Guinea	84	70	6	14	9	16
Ginea-Bissau	91	72	2	6	7	22
Kenya	82	73	4	11	14	15
Lesotho	86	79	3	7	11	13
Liberia	82	65	2	13	16	22
Libyan	32	16	15	30	54	53
Madagascar	92	68	2	11	6	21
Malawi	92	63	3	17	5	19
Mali	75	83	4	2	21	15
Mauritania	82	46	4	16	14	38
Mauritius	24	21	16	26	60	53
Morocco	27	35	46	30	28	34
Mozambique	97	68	1	16	2	15
Namibia	47	32	3	32	50	36
Niger	92	84	0	4	8	12
Nigeria	67	64	7	16	26	20
Reunion	2	16	4	26	94	58
Rwanda	98	86	1	6	2	8
Senegal	87	72	3	10	10	18
Sierra Leone	78	56	4	22	17	23
Somalia	87	61	2	15	11	24
S. Africa	13	11	17	48	70	40
Sudan	84	60	5	10	11	29
Swaziland	78	60	4	16	18	24
Togo	64	72	8	13	28	15
Tunisia	47	25	44	46	10	28
Uganda	85	80	3	8	12	12
Tanzania	89	73	2	10	9	17
Zaire	92	49	2	22	6	29
Zambia	82	65	3	14	15	21

(Contd.)

Country	Agriculture		Industry		Services	
	Women	Men	Women	Men	Women	Men
Zimbabwe	80	62	4	17	16	21
Latin America and Caribbean						
Argentina	2	13	12	41	86	45
Bahamas	2	16	4	26	94	58
Barbados	9	6	18	24	73	69
Belize	2	16	4	26	94	58
Bolivia	28	45	11	22	61	34
Brazil	10	21	19	37	71	42
Chile	2	14	9	27	89	60
Colombia	3	37	20	25	77	38
Costa Rica	4	24	22	28	74	48
Cuba	13	23	21	35	66	41
Dominican Rep.	5	41	3	19	92	40
Ecuador	11	31	11	21	78	48
El Salvador	5	42	18	27	77	32
Guadeloupe	5	13	5	33	90	54
Guatemala	8	60	17	17	74	23
Guyana	7	27	18	26	76	47
Haiti	54	73	9	10	38	16
Honduras	8	66	34	15	58	19
Jamaica	18	41	8	22	75	38
Martinique	16	11	5	29	89	60
Mexico	12	38	35	34	53	28
Netherlands Antilles	2	16	4	26	94	58
Nicaragua	8	52	14	17	79	31
Panama	7	27	7	23	86	50
Paraguay	11	53	16	22	73	25
Peru	26	36	9	22	65	42
Puerto Rico	1	5	31	36	68	58
Surinam	15	15	9	23	76	62
Trinidad and Tobago	4	7	22	48	74	45
Uruguay	2	18	21	33	76	49
Venezuela	4	13	17	35	79	52
Asia and Pacific						
Afghanistan	3	60	85	10	12	30
Armenia	10	23	39	47	50	30
Azerbaijan	36	27	21	35	43	38
Bahrain	0	3	4	39	96	58
Bangladesh	65	68	8	7	27	25

(*Contd.*)

Country	Agriculture		Industry		Services	
	Women	Men	Women	Men	Women	Men
Bhutan	95	89	1	5	4	6
Bruni Daress	1	1	9	32	90	67
Combodia	75	67	11	8	14	25
China	74	67	17	19	10	14
Cyprus	20	9	38	40	42	51
E. Timor	45	76	2	9	53	15
Georgia	24	27	24	38	52	35
Hongkong	2	2	56	48	42	50
India	78	64	10	15	12	20
Indonesia	44	50	16	16	40	35
Iran	69	22	15	40	16	38
Iraq	68	18	9	26	23	56
Israel	4	4	17	37	79	59
Jordan	1	11	7	27	92	62
Kazakhstan	15	28	25	37	60	34
Korea, DPR	41	25	23	45	35	30
Korea. Rep.	31	18	28	38	41	44
Kuwait	0	2	2	36	97	62
Kyrgyzstan	28	35	23	31	49	34
Lao, PDR	76	70	8	10	16	21
Lebanan	16	6	22	32	62	62
Malaysia	31	26	26	24	43	50
Maldives	25	29	63	24	12	46
Mongolia	28	35	21	21	51	44
Myanmar	35	58	25	17	39	26
Nepal	97	91	1	2	2	7
Oman	12	45	39	25	49	30
Pakistan	15	54	23	11	62	35
Philippines	34	56	13	16	53	29
Qatar	0	3	0	30	100	67
S. Arabia	16	34	6	20	79	46
Singapore	1	2	42	35	57	63
Sri Lanka	50	51	14	13	36	35
Syria	60	18	14	39	26	43
Tajikistan	45	37	18	28	37	35
Thailand	64	59	11	18	25	23
Turkey	84	27	6	30	10	43
Turkmenistan	41	34	15	30	44	36
U.A.E.	0	4	7	40	93	56

(*Contd.*)

Country	Agriculture		Industry		Services	
	Women	Men	Women	Men	Women	Men
Uzbekistan	35	34	20	31	45	35
Vietnam	57	59	15	20	28	22
Yemen	45	58	6	14	49	28
Oceania						
Fiji	38	41	9	19	53	37
French Poynesia	6	11	5	29	89	60
Guam	23	55	64	38	12	7
New Caledonia	5	13	5	33	90	54
Popua New Guinea	79	61	7	17	14	22
Samoa	6	11	5	29	89	60
Solomon Islands	5	13	5	33	90	54
Vanuatu	5	12	5	31	89	57

Source: Rao & Latha, *op. cit.*, Table 12, pp. 312-321 (Adapted).

Developed region shows women's less percentage in total labour force in agriculture and industry and more than men in the services. African women have more share in agriculture while industry and services show men's dominance in the labour force. Latin America and Caribbean have larger share of women than men only in the services. Women have more percentage than men in all the three sectors *viz.* agriculture, industry and services in the Asia and Pacific region. Oceania shows women's larger percentage in the services while agriculture and industry have more share of men

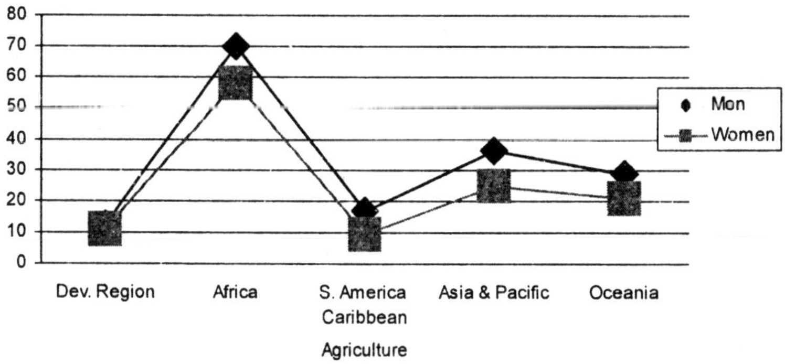

Figure 2.5

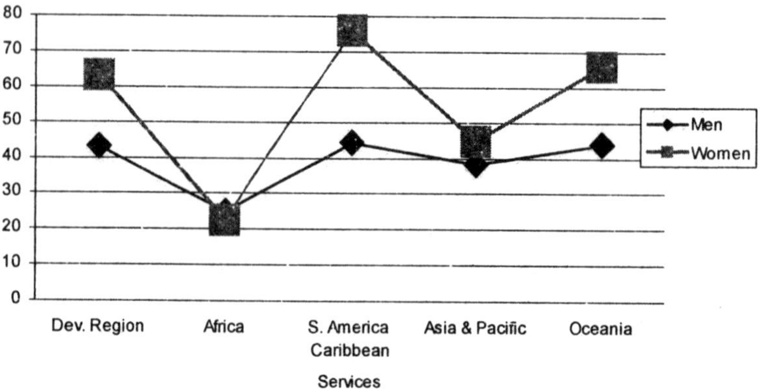

Figure 2.6

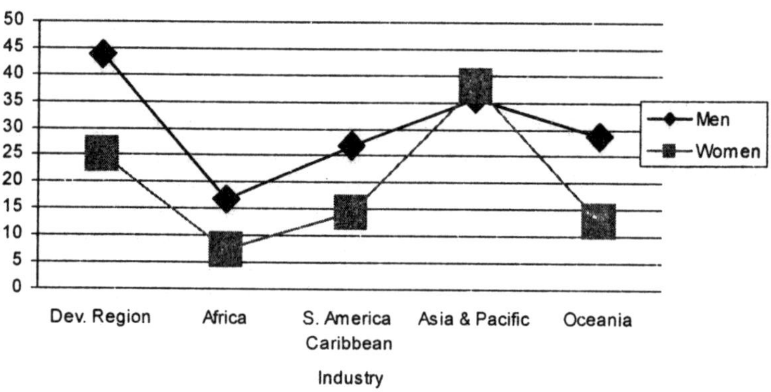

Figure 2.7

than women. Thus Latin America and Caribbean, and Oceania regions have similarity where women's share in total labour force is higher than men in the services.

Women in the Labour Force by Occupations

Basic surmise has been that women are largely in those occupations where remuneration and working conditions are poor. How far this situation has changed in developing regions? Is the percentage share of women increasing or declining *viz-a-viz* men workers? Table 2.2 and analysis throw light on these aspects. It explains

TABLE 2.2: Percentage of Women in Major Occupational Groups

Region	Professional, technical and related work		Administrative and managerial work		Clerical and related work, services		Sales		Production transport and labourer	
	1980	1990	1980	1990	1980	1990	1980	1990	1980	1990
Developed Region										
Eastern Europe	57	56	22	33	64	73	69	66	25	27
Western Europe	42	50	12	18	62	63	48	48	15	16
Other Developed Region	46	44	16	32	65	69	43	41	17	22
Africa										
Northern Africa	24	29	7	9	18	22	3	10	11	10
Sub-Saharan Africa	30	36	8	15	29	37	43	52	13	20
Latin America & Caribbean										
Latin America	47	49	15	23	52	59	39	47	14	17
Caribbean	51	52	22	29	62	62	57	59	18	21
Asia and Pacific										
Eastern Asia	35	43	7	11	41	48	40	42	32	30
S. Eastern Asia	42	48	13	17	40	48	45	53	25	21
Southern Asia	30	32	8	6	15	20	8	8	26	16
Western Asia	30	37	4	7	19	29	6	12	4	7
Oceania	38	41	10	18	42	52	37	53	6	17

Source: Rao & Latha, *op. cit.*, p. 274.

percentage of women workers in the occupational categories of (i) professional, technical and related work, (ii) administrative and managerial work, (iii) clerical, related work and services, (iv) sales and, (v) production, transport, and labour.

Each panel shows percentage share of women in the occupational groups in a region. Professional, technical and related work group shows a higher percentage of women in every region, while their share drops to a low level in these regions for the occupational category of administrative and managerial work. Again women's

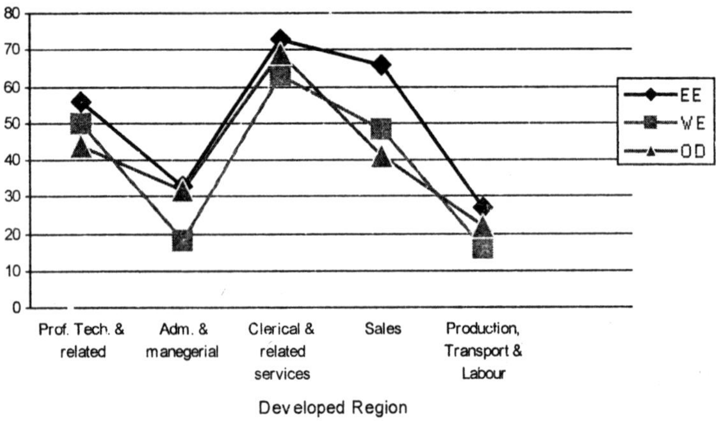

Figure 2.8

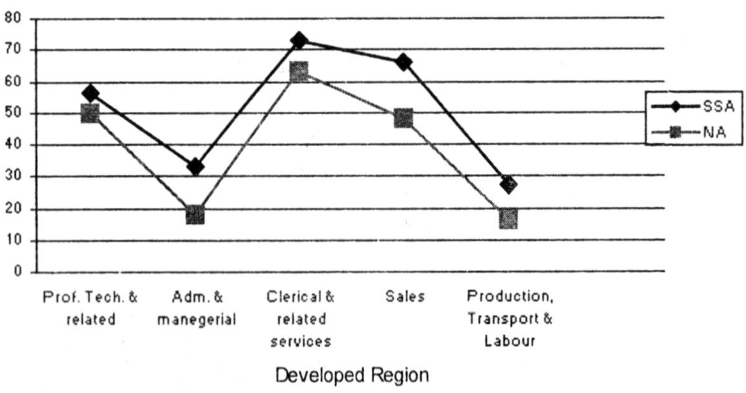

Figure 2.9

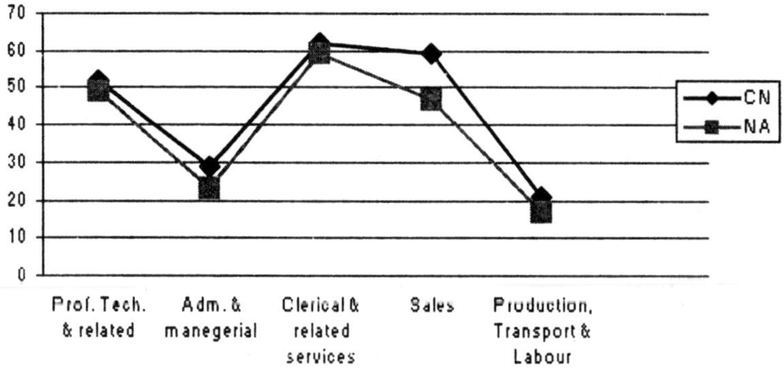

Latin America and Caribbean

Figure 2.10

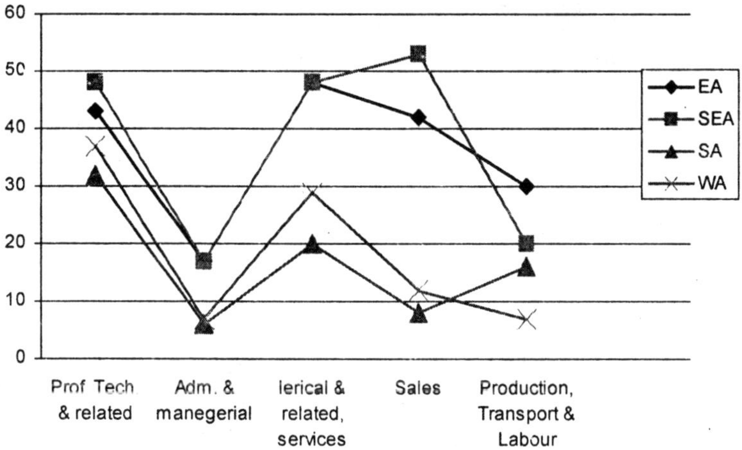

Asia and Pacific

Figure 2.11

percentage has been higher in clerical and related category but declines to a low percentage for sales. Moreover, women have a low participation rate in the occupational group of production, transport and labour. The general behaviour of curves showing women's share by occupational groups in various regions has not been much different. A striking similarity may be observed for women's representation in various occupations, though regions are diverse in nature and also in the matter of socio-economic development.

However a comparative picture is required to evaluate the place of women *vis-à-vis* men in various occupational groups in developed and developing regions.

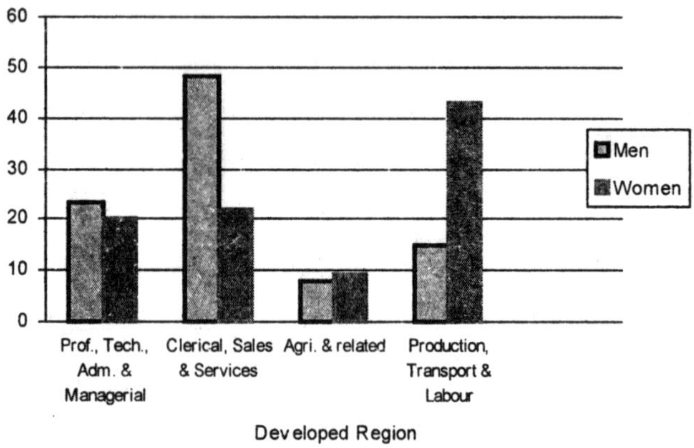

Figure 2.12

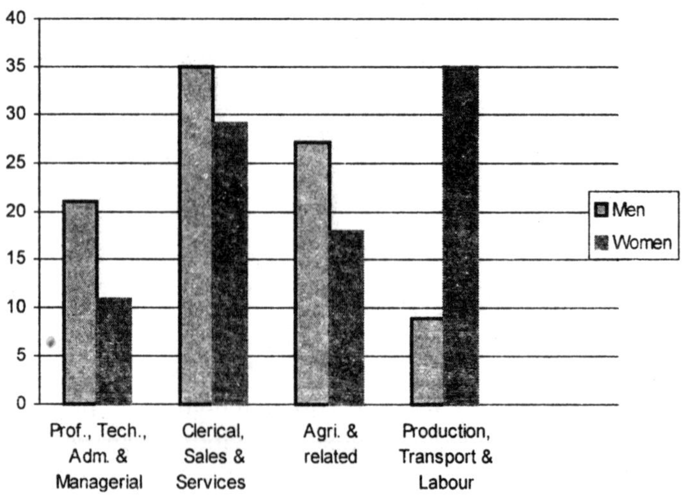

Figure 2.13

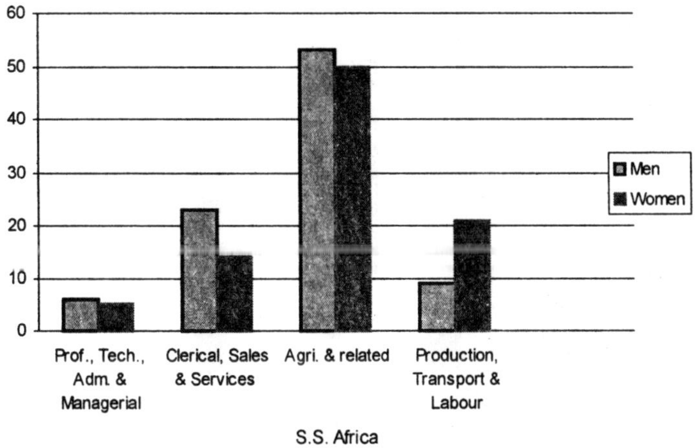

Figure 2.14

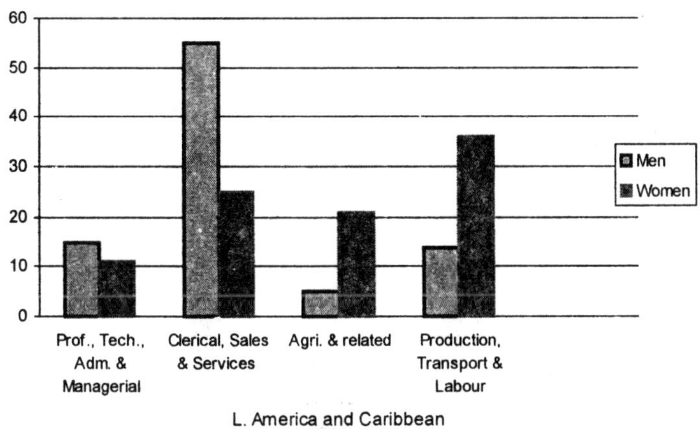

Figure 2.15

Out of four major occupational groups, women's percentage is more than men in the occupational groups of professional, technical, administrative and managerial category and, clerical, sales and services in developed region. While men have larger percentage than women in the categories of agriculture and related work, and production, transport and labourers in the region.

Women in the Northern Africa and West Asia have dominance

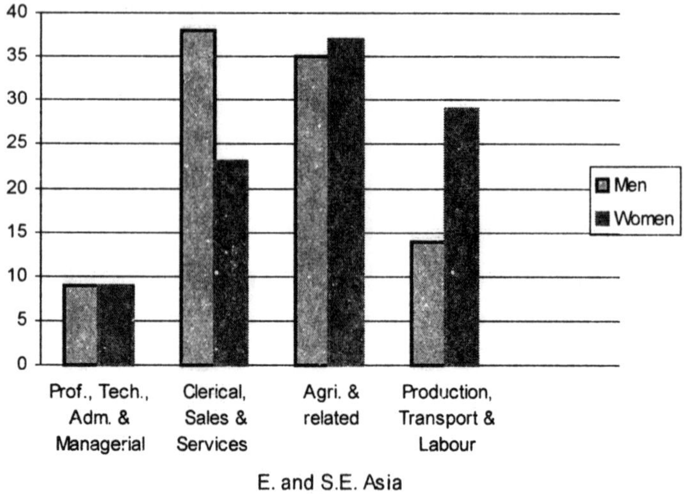

Figure 2.16

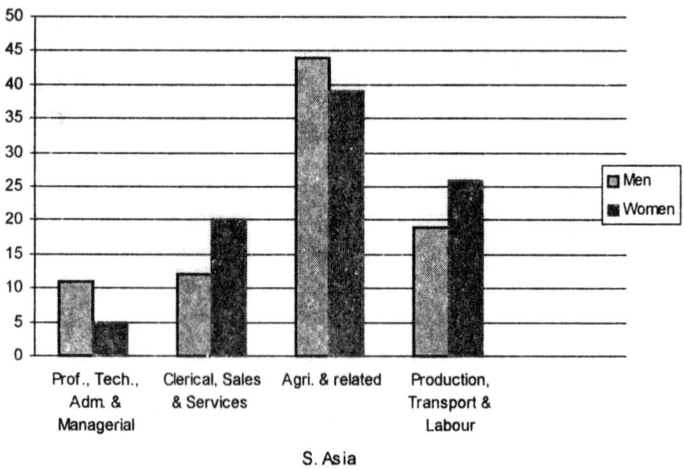

Figure 2.17

in all groups except production, transport and labourer. While sub-Saharan Africa shows the same pattern of women's percentage distribution as it is in the Northern Africa and West Asia.

Latin America and Caribbean region has women's percent distribution by occupational groups similar to developed region.

TABLE 2.3: Per cent Rate of Unemployment by Sex 1991-92

Countries where unemployment rate of women is:	
Higher than men	Lower than men
Developed Region	
Austria, Luxembourg	Australia
Belgium, Poland	Canada
Czechoslovakia, Portugal	Finland
Denmark, Romania	Ireland
France, Spain	Malta
Germany Fed. Rep., Switzerland	New Zealand
Greece, Yugoslavia (Former)	Norway
Hungary	Sweden
Iceland	UK
Italy	USA
Japan	
Latvia	
Latin America and Caribbean	
Argentina, Bahamas, Barbados, Bolivia, Chile, Costa Rica, Ecuador, French Guiana, Jamaica, Mexico, Netherland Antilles, Nicaragua, Panama, Peru, Trinidad & Tobago, Uruguay	Brazil, Elsalvador, Paraguay, Puerto Rico, Venezuela
Asia and Pacific	
China, Israel, Pakistan, Philippines, Sri Lanka, Syria, Thailand	Hongkong, Korea (Republic), Macau, Singapore, Turkey

Source: *ILO Yearbook of Labour Statistics*, Geneva, ILO, various issues.

East and South-East Asia has a different pattern of percentage distribution of male and female workers across various occupational groups. Women dominate in the clerical, sales and services, and agriculture and related work occupational groups. While men and women have equal percentage distribution in the category of professional, technical, administrative and managerial work.

Lastly, women have higher percentage in the occupational groups of professional, technical, administrative and managerial work; and agriculture and related work in South Asia.

Thus women's per cent share by occupational groups differs across the region, though developed region, and Latin America and Caribbean region have similarities.

Women in the Informal Sector

Informal sector has emerged as major provider of employment in most of developing countries. Women are generally in the secondary segment of the dual labour market and largely fall in the informal sector. "Activities in the sector are an updated representation of the primitive accumulation process in the urban centers. Access to factors of production and technology is determined by social relations and heritage, and family and friendship more than by the market system and prices" (Aboagye & Gozo, 1986).

The employment of women in the informal sector varies from region to region. These are African countries where informal sector is more significant from the view point of employment in general and women's employment in particular. The situation of employment of women in the informal sector may be seen from Table 2.4 showing women's percentage share in various economic activities, e.g. manufacturing, transport and services falling in the informal sector of various countries.

TABLE 2.4: Percent Distribution of Women in the Informal Sector

Country	Year	Manufac-turing	Transport	Services	Total
Africa					
Burundi	1990	30	0	26	28
Congo	1984	12	0	63	46
Egypt	1986	1	0	5	3
Gambia	1983	13	4	54	44
Mali	1990	49	0	35	40
Zambia	1986	41	11	65	59
Latin America and Caribbean					
Brazil	1990	8	1	52	41
Costa Rica	1984	17	2	15	15
Honduras	1990	58	3	57	55
Jamaica	1988	15	4	67	53
Mexico	1992	28	1	35	32
Uruguay	1985	32	3	37	34
Venezuela	1992	37	2	41	34

(Contd.)

Country	Year	Manufac-turing	Transport	Services	Total
Asia and Pacific					
Indonesia	1985	51	1	52	48
Iraq	1987	7	0	7	5
Korea, Rep.	1989	25	8	34	31
Malaysia	1986	54	2	43	42
Qatar	1986	0	0	0	0
Syria	1991	5	0	1	1
Thailand	1990	44	3	58	48
Turkey	1985	9	1	4	4
Fiji	1986	18	1	30	22

Source: Rao & Latha, op. cit., pp. 294-95.

Women's share in the total informal sector labour force exceeds fifty per cent in Zambia, Honduras, Jamaica; while it is between 40 and 50 per cent in Congo, Gambia, Mali, Brazil, Indonesia, Malaysia and Thailand.

TABLE 2.5: Analysis of Women's Distribution in the Informal Sector

Percentiles of distribution	Countries
0-10	Egypt, Iraq, Qatar, Syria, Turkey
10-20	Costa Rica
20-30	Burundi, Fiji
30-40	Mexico, Uruguay, Venezuela, Korea
40-50	Congo, Gambia, Mali, Brazil, Indonesia, Malaysia, Thailand
50-60	Zambia, Honduras, Jamaica
60 & >	Nil

The concentration of women in the informal sector is, of course, in the region of Africa. However, Latin America has a significant position. Largely populated countries of Asia, such as, Indonesia also have a significant presence of women workers in their informal sector.

Informal sector is, therefore, major provider of women employment in developing countries in general and African region in particular. Statistics also indicate that those countries where Islam is a predominant religion have less percentage of women in the informal sector. However, Indonesia and Malaysia may be seen as exception in this regard.

Employment Status of Women

One of the indicators of economic empowerment of working women may be the employment status which reflects the relative position of women in the world of work.

Women by status of employment may be classified into three major categories namely (i) employers, own-account workers, (ii) unpaid family workers and , (iii) employees or wage employment.

Available data given in Table 2.6 presents some striking results. For example when data showing per cent distribution of women in each category of employment are subjected to mean measurements, average for women employers, own-account workers comes to 29.2 per cent, 32.4 per cent, 27.6 per cent, 17.4 per cent and 22.9 per cent for developed region, Africa, Latin America and Caribbean, Asia and Pacific, and Oceania respectively. It means Africa has the highest percentage distribution of women in the category of employers cum own-account workers followed by developed region, Latin America and Caribbean, Oceania and, Asia and Pacific.

TABLE 2.6: Distribution of Women Workers by Employment Status—1990

Countries	Employers, own-account workers	Unpaid family workers	Employees
Developed Region			
Australia	32	59	43
Austria	31	75	41
Belgium	27	85	40
Canada	35	80	45
Croatia	36	74	43
Czech Rep.	24	76	48
Denmark	16	97	48

(*Contd.*)

Countries	Employers, own-account workers	Unpaid family workers	Employees
Finland	34	38	49
France	22	82	43
Germany Fed. Rep.	25	85	41
Greece	21	76	35
Hungary	31	82	47
Ireland	11	37	35
Italy	24	63	36
Japan	31	82	38
Luxembourg	24	84	35
Netherlands	30	91	37
New Zealand	26	66	47
Norway	24	67	47
Poland	27	76	45
Portugal	42	60	41
Romania	58	67	42
Slovakia	47	66	21
Slovenia	27	62	47
Spain	24	62	33
Sweden	26	67	50
USA	33	76	46
Africa			
Algeria	2	6	10
Benin	47	40	21
Botswana	47	35	36
Burkina Faso	16	66	13
Burundi	53	60	13
Cameroon	39	70	10
Cape Verde	46	54	32
C. African Rep.	52	55	10
Congo	60	65	16
Cote d' Ivoire	17	62	7
Djibouti	28	22	33
Egypt	20	62	16
Equi. Guinea	17	74	11
Ethiopia	28	67	35
Gambia	44	64	20
Ghana	56	63	24
Guinea	19	60	43
Guinea-Bissau	1	4	10

(*Contd.*)

Countries	Employers, own-account workers	Unpaid family workers	Employees
Lesotho	24	39	38
Liberia	47	65	13
Malawi	57	58	13
Mali	15	53	17
Mauritania	23	38	15
Mauritius	13	48	33
Morocco	11	31	18
Mozambique	41	82	12
Namibia	49	69	32
Niger	17	24	15
Nigeria	36	46	15
Rwanda	33	70	15
Sao Tome and Principe	26	54	32
Seychelles	15	60	38
Sierra Leone	24	74	20
Swaziland	42	59	30
Togo	48	54	15
Tunisia	17	49	17
Uganda	32	74	19
Tanzania	47	88	17
Zambia	55	54	16
Latin America and Caribbean			
Bahamas	37	72	48
Barbados	31	67	45
Bolivia	49	79	27
Brazil	29	46	37
Chile	24	42	33
Colombia	33	74	41
Costa Rica	18	34	32
Cuba	7	5	33
Dominica	30	50	44
Dominicom Rep.	20	43	35
Ecuador	22	27	31
El Salvador	56	58	38
Guatemala	25	21	27
Haiti	38	37	44
Mexico	14	11	28
Netherlands Antilles	21	80	38
Panama	14	15	38

(*Contd.*)

Countries	Employers, own-account workers	Unpaid family workers	Employees
Paraguay	43	24	41
Peru	40	64	32
Puerto Rico	14	73	40
St. Vincent	27	42	37
Surinam	29	42	41
Trinidad and Tobago	23	54	36
Uruguay	25	40	35
US Virgin Islands	25	53	49
Venezuela	23	34	35
Asia and Pacific			
Bahrain	1	8	12
Bangladesh	5	6	17
Brunei Daress.	19	55	23
Cyprus	34	83	37
Hongkong	19	77	40
Indonesia	27	66	32
Iran	4	43	10
Iraq	6	50	11
Israel	25	72	43
Jordan	1	4	9
Kazakhstan	70	91	46
Korea, DPR	27	69	29
Korea, Rep.	27	87	38
Kuwait	1	4	21
Macau	17	86	43
Malaysia	24	64	34
Maldives	22	29	17
Nepal	36	55	15
Pakistan	4	33	10
Philippines	30	53	36
Qatar	1	4	10
Singapore	18	77	42
Sri Lanka	18	56	35
Syria	3	5	15
Thailand	27	64	42
Turkey	11	69	18
UAE	1	9	5
Yomen	15	69	6

(*Contd.*)

Countries	Employers, own-account workers	Unpaid family workers	Employees
Oceania			
American Samoa	22	68	42
Cook Islands	32	26	36
Fiji	10	20	26
Guam	41	55	42
Marshall Islands	29	28	26
New Caledonia	31	75	39
N. Mariana Islands	25	54	43
Palau	23	50	37
Samoa	9	8	37
Tonga	7	4	31

Source: Adapted from Rao & Latha, op. cit., T. 12, pp. 312-22.

Similarly percentage distribution of women in the category of unpaid family workers shows highest mean value for developed region followed by Africa, Asia and Pacific, Latin America and Caribbean, and Oceania. While the mean value of the percentage of women as employees has been highest for developed region followed by Latin America and Caribbean, Oceania, Asia and Pacific, and Africa.

Variations measured in terms of percentage show minimum in the per cent distribution of women workers pertaining to employers/own-account workers for developed region and maximum in case of Asia and Pacific. The same is true for women as employees. Similarly it is maximum and minimum for the category of unpaid family workers in developed region and Oceania respectively. It is well-known that variation and stability are opposite to each other meaning thereby maximum variation reflects least stability and its vice-versa.

Correlation analysis of data given in Table 2.7 shows negligible relationship between women employers/own-account workers and unpaid family workers, employers and employees and unpaid family workers and employees in the developed region. Table 2.7 shows the degree of relationships for each region.

TABLE 2.7: Karl Pearson's Coefficient of Correlation for Employment Status of Women

Region	Correlation		
	Employers/own-account and unpaid family workers	Employer/own-account workers and employees	Unpaid family workers and employees
Developed	–0.09 (0.0081)	–0.13 (0.0169)	0.04 (0.0016)
Africa	0.42 (0.1764)	0.07 (0.0049)	0.02 (0.0004)
Latin America and Caribbean	0.70 (0.4900)	0.67 (0.4489)	0.72 (0.5184)
Asia and Pacific	0.41 (0.1681)	0.12 (0.0144)	0.36 (0.1296)
Oceania	0.59 (0.3481)	0.39 (0.1521)	0.60 (0.3600)

Note: Value in parentheses show r^2.

Only regions which show significant relationships between various categories of employment have been Latin America and Caribbean, and Oceania. However correlation analysis is only indicative in nature and does not amount to causal relationship.

Unemployment of Women

Due to under reporting and lack of proper accounting of women work, employment and unemployment figures of women have the cloud of suspicion. Women's unemployment is generally high particularly in developing countries. However, the available statistics present the following comparative picture of unemployment by sex.

There are very few countries where women's unemployment rate is lower than that of men. On the contrary, women have higher unemployment rate than men in most of the countries.

Sum-up

Gender inequality in employment is a well established and

documented fact. Societal attitude and attributes are mainly responsible for gender discrimination in employment, at least in developing countries. Young women have larger share in employment and hence age-based discrimination against women has also been noticed. It is true particularly in private sector of a developing economy. Moreover, similar trend has also been observed in the informal sector where most of women find employment. Such and other discriminatory practices are still prevalent and these may be attributed to societal attitude.

Women are largely concentrated in low-paid jobs where advancement is either negligible or non-existent. It leads to segregation of occupation and hence dissimilarity indices have been developed. Since women are considered immobile in terms of time, energy and space it also becomes a cause to discriminate them.

Dual labour market theory is based on the presumption of segmentation. Labour market divided into primary and secondary sectors has women in secondary jobs where organizational hierarchy does not exists. Thus advancement opportunities are negligible and working conditions are generally poor.

The encouraging note regarding women has been their increased share in total labour force. On the contrary, men's economic activity rate has generally declined. It does not auger well. An increased share of women in employment by displacing, if not replacing, men workers may not be taken as a good sign.

Data disaggregated at occupational level of women reflect striking similarities in different regions of the world. They have a relatively higher percentage in the professional, technical and related occupations which drops to a lower level for the occupational group of administrative and managerial positions in every region. Again, a peak is attained in the category of clerical, sales and services. They have a low representation in the occupational group of production, transport and workers. By and large, these trends reflect universal phenomenon. The only occupation where women dominate has been the clerical, sales and services.

Women are not uniformly distributed in the informal sector in various regions. African, Latin American and Asian particularly south-east Asian countries have significant employment of women in their informal sector. Africa tops the list in this regard.

Women employment is generally categorized into: (i) employers, own-account workers (ii) family labour, unpaid and (iii) employees. Women's contribution in the secondary category has turned out highest in every region. It creates the problem of accounting of women work which is generally under-reported and sometimes misreported.

REFERENCES

Barron, R.D. and Norris, G.M. (1974), "Sexual Divisions and the Dual Labour Market", paper presented at the BSA annual conference, mimeo.

Jha, U.S., Mehta, A. and Menon, L. (1998), " The Informal Sector: An Appraisal of the Concept" in JASPA (ed.), The Challenge of Employment and Basic Needs in Africa, Nairobi, Oxford University Press, p. 267.

3

Women Workers in India—A Bird's Eyeview

Indian economy has a significant presence of women not only as home makers but also as workers. Since long women have been the backbone of rural sector. Agricultural activities except ploughing have important contribution of women as they perform all major work like sowing, weeding, manuring and harvesting. Even the post harvest work, that is, storage is considered as one of the responsibility of women in rural sector. However, women in agriculture are either unpaid family workers or wage employees. They are rarely employers or own-account workers in agricultural sector. Similarly allied activities in the rural sector are largely handled and managed by women. For example, milch cattle such as cows, buffaloes and goats are generally managed by them, though grazing responsibility falls on children. Women are exclusively responsible for managing and handling dung either for manure or fuel purpose. These activities are performed by women in rural setting besides their normal activities of cooking, bearing and rearing of children and taking care of their family. Their reproductive and productive roles are so inter-twined that these are not only inseparable but the latter is undermined. No accounting of women's unpaid productive activities has been done in the rural economy.

Women are in large number in the agricultural sector as daily labourers or wage employees. They are hired largely during the sowing, winnoing and harvesting times. Paddy cultivation has significant employment or engagement of women workers in rural India, particularly during sowing and harvesting seasons. Women as hired labour may also be seen in some cash crops. However family labour dominates in either case.

Cottage industries generally thrive upon female labour since largely women work in this sector. Moreover, women in the category of own-account workers or employers are common in this category. Since most of cottage industries produce articles to be used in households such as pickles, papads, candles, spices and lentils etc. which fall in the domain of domestic work or chores, women easily take up such work as cottage industry. Even employment in this sector is generally favoured to women due to their suitability and background. Traditional handicrafts also favour women as they do such work in their spare time to contribute to family earnings. They are generally paid wages on the basis of piece-rate and have no regular employment.

Women, therefore, find work mostly in the agricultural and informal sector where employment is either occupational or menial. Such jobs carry low payment without advancement and no security.

In the formal sector women have opening in certain occupations like primary teaching, front office jobs such as counselling and reception, housekeeping, typing etc. Again they are favoured for low paid jobs with negligible promotion opportunities. Discriminatory attitude based on sex and age is prevailing in the Indian society.

Women in Rural Sector

Women are largely employed in the rural sector in general and agriculture in particular. It is estimated that around 80 per cent of all women workers is employed in agriculture while of total female labour their share is around 87 per cent (Arya, 2000). Stratification of women employment is totally dependent on the social structure prevalent in rural India and a number of social and legal factors are responsible. For example, women generally do not hire land nor have land titles due to customs and traditions. Moreover, rural labour households have experienced an increase over the period in the total rural households. Its role in affecting the size of rural women employment may not be undermined. National percentage of labour households in total rural household

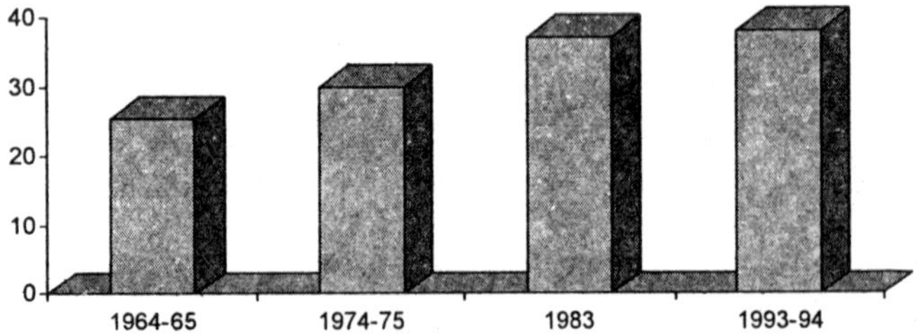

Figure 3.1: Percentage of Labour Households in Total Rural Household.

shows an increasing trend from sixties while a slight decline has been noticed in the early nineties. A decennial increase in percentage may be noticed since it was 25.4 per cent in 1964, 30.2 per cent in 1974, 37.3 per cent in 1983 and 38.3 per cent in 1993 where a continuous growth has taken place. However increasing trend in the share of labour household in total rural households may not be considered as a positive sign since it reflects deterioration in the rural hierarchy.

Andhra Pradesh, Bihar, Gujarat, Kerala, Madhya Pradesh, Tamil Nadu and West Bengal registered a sharp increase in the percentage of labour households in total households. Severe drought conditions had repercussions and resulted in an increase not only in the percentage share of labour households but also increased the percentage of labour households with cultivated land (Labour Bureau, 1998).

What was its impact on the female but earning population of rural labour households? In comparison to males earner population ratio of women declined significantly during the period. It was 36.4 per cent in1964-65 and rose to 41.6 per cent in the next decade but started declining from 32.5 per cent in 1983 to 30.3 per cent in 1993-94. On the contrary, men's percentage increased from 55.5 per cent in 1964-65 to 56.1 per cent in 1974-75. It declined to 54.5 per cent in 1983 but increased to 57.1 per cent in 1993-94. Therefore the trends have been divergent. Similar trend has been observed in the percentage of wage earners to total earners in rural labour households (Unni, 1999).

Women employment measured in terms of annual full days has dissimilarity vis-à-vis men employment in rural labour households.

TABLE 3.1: Employment of Wage Employed Men and Women in Rural Labour H.H.

(Full Days p.a.)

Year	Men	Women
1964-65	277	199
1974-75	250	185
1983-84	286	233
1993-94	305	265
Average	279.5	220.5
S.D.	22.87	35.87
C.V.	8.18	16.27

Source: Row 1-4 Unni, J., 1999, *op. cit.*, Table 7. Last three rows are computed.

Average annual days for men and women are 279.5 and 220.5 respectively which show disparity in their employment. Moreover, men have less variation or more stability in the number of working days and women have more variation or less stability in that matter. Women, therefore, face more discrimination in employment than men in rural labour households, that too, in the matter of employment.

Agricultural earnings of men and women workers in rural labour households differ and show disparity on the basis of sex.

There are two things obvious from Table 3.2. Firstly, men's wage earnings have been more than wage earnings of women in rural labour households. Secondly, wage earnings of both men and women have increased over the period. Though women wage

TABLE 3.2: Real Agricultural Wage Earnings in Rural Labour Households

(at 1960-61 prices)

Workers	Year			
	1964-65	1974-75	1983	1993-94
Men	1.0	0.9	1.0	1.9
Women	0.6	0.6	0.7	1.3

Source: (Adopted) Unni, J., 1999, *op. cit.*, Table 9, pp. 110-111.

TABLE 3.3: Distribution of Workers by Status of Employment

(in per cent)

Year	Men workers			Women workers		
	Self-employed	Regular	Casual	Self-employed	Regular	Casual
1977-78	62.8	10.6	26.6	62.1	2.8	35.1
1983	60.5	10.3	29.2	61.9	2.8	35.3
1987-88	58.6	10.0	31.4	60.8	3.7	35.3
1989-90	59.7	9.8	30.5	60.9	2.8	36.3
1990-91	55.7	12.8	31.5	58.6	3.8	37.6
1991	59.5	9.2	31.3	56.8	3.1	40.1
1992	60.8	8.3	30.9	59.1	3.2	37.7
1993	59.1	7.9	33.0	58.5	2.3	39.2
1993-94	57.9	8.3	33.8	58.5	2.8	38.7

Source: Unni, J., 1999, *op. cit.*, Table 1, p. 100.

earnings have doubled and also increased more than their counterparts during the period, still they get only 68 per cent of male wage earnings. Wage differentials thus show disparity or dissimilarity between male and female workers and the latter are discriminated against in terms of wages as well. It is confirmed by average daily wage earned in rural households between men and women. As per the report of the Labour Bureau, their national average has been Rs.21.52 and Rs.15.33 for men and women (Labour Bureau, 1998). Women's daily wage earning happens to be very close to the minimum of prevailing minimum wages, i.e. 14.15 to 33 in 1993, while men's wage rate has been much higher than the minimum wages.

Lastly, distribution of workers by status of employment shows disparity between men and women workers in the rural sector.

The pattern of workers' distribution by employment status has been the same in rural sector i.e. around 60 per cent in the category of self-employed, 30-40 per cent as casual workers followed by regulars. The sex factor does not affect distribution pattern of workers by employment status. However, women have much lower percentage than men in the category of regular workers.

All the facts and figures do show that women are worse-off as compared to men in rural sector of the country. It leads to agreement with the study which concludes that female marginalization has taken place in Indian economy and hence women have low work participation rates, higher unemployment rate, casualisation of female labour and, shift to low paid occupations (Parthasarthy *et al.*, 1999). The sexism in employment has been generalized and women are its victim since long (Sharma, 1999).

Non-Farm Rural Employment

In non-farm rural sector a dramatic change in employment took place in certain sectors from mid-seventies to eighties such as construction, transport-cum-storage-cum-communication etc. while growth in agriculture and livestock slowed down. However, the trend was reversed in the post-liberalization as the phase of restructuring in rural sector seemed to be over.

Employment of men in non-agricultural rural sector has risen from 16.8 per cent in 1972-73 to 25.9 per cent in 1993-94 while women registered an increase till 1987-88 and a decline in 1993-94. The percentage share of women in total non-agricultural rural employment has been less than men during the periods. Moreover, women's share in terms of the percentage of male workers has declined during the period. They accounted for 61.3 per cent of male employment in 1972-73 and 1977-78 which declined to 60 per cent in the next two consecutive periods and finally decreased to just 54 per cent of total male employment in non-agricultural rural sector. Therefore the situation of women employment in non-farm rural sector has deteriorated over the years. Discrimination against women workers has been more in the non-agricultural rural sector than what it is in agricultural rural sector in India.

Women Workers in the Formal Sector

Women employment in the formal or organized sector has improved since independence due to concerted efforts made at different levels. The share of women in the organized sector has been low but increasing gradually in India. It was, for example, only 61 per cent of the total women workers in the country in 1971 but grew to 14

TABLE 3.3: Distribution of Rural Workers by Sectors and Sex

(in per cent)

Sector	Male					Female				
	1972-73	1977-78	1983-84	1987-88	1993-94	1972-73	1977-78	1983-84	1987-88	1993-94
Primary	83.2	80.6	77.5	74.5	74.1	89.7	88.1	87.5	84.7	86.2
Mining and Quarrying	0.4	0.5	0.6	0.7	0.7	0.2	0.2	0.3	0.4	0.4
Manufacturing	5.7	6.4	7.0	7.4	7.0	4.7	5.9	6.4	6.9	7.0
Construction	1.6	1.7	2.2	3.7	3.2	1.1	0.6	0.7	2.7	0.9
Secondary	7.8	8.8	10.0	12.1	11.2	6.0	6.8	8.7	10.0	8.4
Trade Hotelling	3.1	4.0	4.4	5.1	5.5	1.5	2.0	1.9	2.1	2.1
Transport and Communication	1.0	1.2	1.7	2.0	2.2	0.1	0.1	0.1	0.1	–
Services	4.8	5.3	6.1	6.2	7.0	2.8	3.0	2.8	3.0	3.4
Tertiary	9.0	10.6	12.5	13.4	14.7	4.3	5.1	4.8	5.3	5.6
Total (non-agri.)	16.8	19.4	22.5	25.5	25.9	10.3	11.9	13.5	15.3	14.0

Source: Chadha, G.K., "Non-Farm Employment in Rural Areas: How well can Female Workers Compete?", in Papola, T.S. and Sharma, A.N. (Eds.), *op. cit.*, Table 3, pp. 150-151.

per cent during the next decade (Arya, 2000, p. 241). The situation has improved but still a lot is to be done to give women a right place in the formal sector.

The ratio of female to male employment has been very low in India, particularly in the formal sector. The sector has experienced jobless growth not only in India but in other countries as well. That explains why workers expecially women had to take refuge in the informal sector where low payment and poor working conditions make the bargain worse. In contrast, formal sector provides better remuneration and security of employment.

Formal sector may be studied in terms of public and private sector as India has mixed economy.

Women Employment in the Public Sector

In a mixed economy like India, public sector is envisaged to play a leading role in the matter of, *inter alia*, employment. It is true in the case of India that public sector has a larger share in employment in the formal sector irrespective of sex. Of total workers in the formal sector, 70 per cent are employed in the public sector. Similarly 71 per cent of total male workers and 60 per cent of total female workers in the organized sector are employed in the public sector. However disparity between men and women workers could not be dispensed with even in the public sector employment. Distribution of male-female workers in the public sector in the form of ratio of women per thousand men workers surprisingly shows more disparity as it is 157 women workers per 1000 male

TABLE 3.5: Number of Men-Women Workers in the Public Sector, 1996

Sector	Male workers	Female workers	Total workers	Per cent of women
Primary	1,418	115	1,533	7.5
Secondary	3,625	218	3,843	5.7
Tertiary	11,751	2,303	14,054	16.4
Total	16,795	2,635	19,429	13.6

Source: Ministry of Labour, *Employment Review*, Government of India, 1996 (Percentage computed).

TABLE 3.6: Distribution of Women Workers by Industrial Sectors, 1996

Industry	No. of women workers ('000)	Total workers (lakhs)	Per cent of total
Agriculture	49.2	540.4	9.10
Mining	65.5	992.7	6.60
Manufacturing	119.5	1,737.5	6.88
Electricity	36.7	946.3	3.88
Construction	61.4	1,158.7	5.30
Trade	15.4	162	9.51
Transport	157.6	3,092.0	5.10
Finance	169.1	1,279.6	13.22
Community Ser.	1,960.5	9,520	20.59
Total	2,634.5	19,429.3	13.56

Source: Ministry of Labour, *op. cit.*

workers in the public sector, a ratio which is lower than the national ratio at 188 per thousand men workers in 1996. So disparity between male and female workers exists and large enough in the public sector in India.

Women have a low percentage of 13.6 per cent of total workers in the public sector. When it is disaggregated at sectoral level it comes out as low as 7.5 per cent, 5.7 per cent and 16.5 per cent for primary, secondary and tertiary sectors.

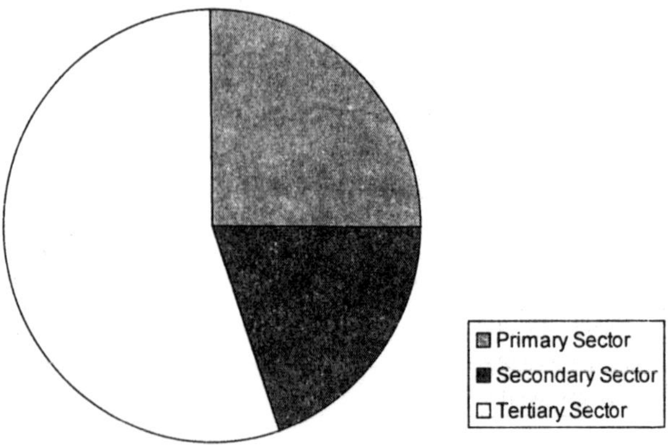

Figure 3.2

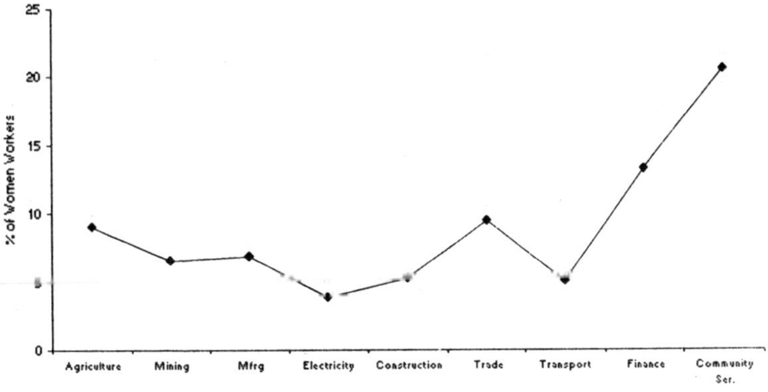

Figure 3.3: Percent Distribution of Women by Industry in the Public Sector.

Hence women's share in various sector in the public sector is by no means significant. However women are relatively more in the tertiary sector followed by primary and secondary sectors respectively.

Women's employment by industrial sectors, given below, shows that they have relatively higher percentage in community, finance and trade sectors followed by agriculture.

The situation of women employment can not be said satisfactory in any of the industrial activity since their share varies between 3.9 per cent and 20.6 per cent of total employees in the public sector. Special drive for enhancing women employment should be initiated by the government if employment inequality between men and women is to be reduced, if not eliminated.

Women Employment in Private Sector

Employment of women in private sector has been quantitatively less than public sector. Another significant difference between public and private sector in the matter of women employment is that the former has more women in its tertiary sector while the latter in the primary and secondary sectors. Following is situation of women employment in private sector of Indian economy (Table 3.7).

It is primary sector where women have significant size in employment, i.e. 43.5 per cent, while their percentages in secondary

TABLE 3.7: Sectoral Distribution of Women Workers in Private sector

Sector	No. of men workers ('000)	No. of women workers ('000)	Total	Per cent of women in total	women as per cent of men
Primary	580	446	1,026	43.46	76.89
Secondary	4,382	762	5,144	14.81	17.38
Tertiary	1,757	584	2,341	24.94	33.23
Total	6,720	1,792	8,512	21.05	26.66

Source: Op. cit.

and tertiary sectors are 14.8 and 24.9 respectively. It is the over all share of women which actually shows that women are not even one-fourth of total employees.

Women as percentage of men employment are around three-quarter in the primary sector where the gap between men and women workers is very small. However, secondary sector has women just 17.4 per cent of total men workers. Similarly, women are one-third of men workers in tertiary sector. In total, women as percentage of men workers are around one-quarter, reflecting a poor position of women workers in private sector of the economy.

Comparing the two from the viewpoint of women employment, private sector turns out better as it has more percentage of women, than what it is in public sector, in primary, secondary and tertiary activities. Moreover the over all share of women has been 13.6 per cent and 21 per cent in public and private sectors respectively. Therefore, women are better placed in the matter of employment, in the private sector. However their position at disaggregated level, that is, by industrial activity has been shown in Table 3.8.

Agriculture and community development are two sectors in which women have significant presence, otherwise they are worse-off in every other industrial activity in private sector. A comparative position of women employment by industrial activity in public and private sector has been given in Figure 3.4.

Women workers have less percentage of total in the private sector, compared with public sector, in electricity, construction trade, and finance while they are better placed in agriculture,

TABLE 3.8: Women Employment in Private Sector by Industrial Activity, 1996

Industry	No. of women workers ('000)	No. of total workers ('000)	Per cent of total
Agriculture	429.3	918.7	46.7
Mining	16.4	107.3	15.3
Manufacturing	756.8	5,049.2	15.0
Electricity	1.1	41.8	2.6
Construction	4.0	53.2	7.5
Trade	25.1	316.9	7.9
Transport	4.5	59.9	7.5
Finance	39.0	306.2	12.7
Community Ser.	515.7	1,658.3	31.1
Total	1,791.9	8,511.6	21.0

Source: Ministry of Labour, *Employment Review*, Government of India, various issues.

mining, manufacturing, construction, transport and community development. Hence women workers have better dispersal by industrial activity in private sector, while larger size of employment they have in public sector.

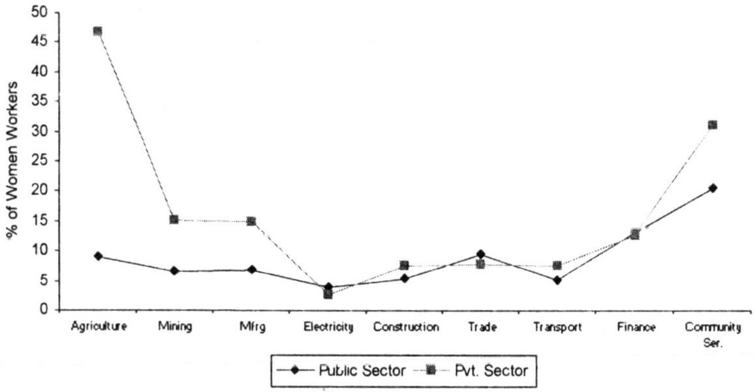

Figure 3.4: Comparative Position of Women Workers by Industrial Activity.

Wage Differentials

Equal pay for equal work is the main issue for which international organizations like the ILO have been striving since long. ILO's convention on Equal Remuneration (No. 100) was the milestone and its threads were picked up by other bodies and legislations in various countries. Dissimilarity indices have also been developed to measure the extent of discrimination against women in terms of wage differentials. Despite sustained efforts made at different levels, wage differential still persists and indicates discrimination against women workers in most of the countries including India (Jose, 1987).

How far wages are discriminatory for women workers a glimpse of it has been given in Table 3.9.

Table 3.9 shows that wage differentials exist in various industries and sectors as well. However, public sector has less disparity in wages in its various industries as compared to the private sector. The extent of differential in wages is more at sectoral levels in the private sector. Figure 3.5 makes it more clear.

Disparity between wages of men and women exists in both the sectors but it is larger in the private sector. Male workers get much more wages than female workers in both public and private sectors but difference is relatively larger in the latter. It reflects that women are generally in low-paid jobs with little promotional avenues and indicates marginalization of women workers in Indian economy.

TABLE 3.9: Wages by Sex in the Public and Private Sectors

Industry	Public sector			Private sector		
	Male	Female	M/F	Male	Female	M/F
Agriculture	1,145	1,133	1.01	1,324	900	1.47
Manufacturing	1,303	1,021	1.28	1,445	897	1.61
Services	1,101	864	1.27	1,314	830	1.58
Administration	1,105	942	1.17	1,031	786	1.31
All	1,138	927	1.23	1,279	800	1.60

Source: Srivastava, N., 1999, "Striving for a Toe-Hold: Women in the Organised Sector" in Papola, T.S. and Sharma, A.N. (Eds.), *op. cit.*, p. 185.

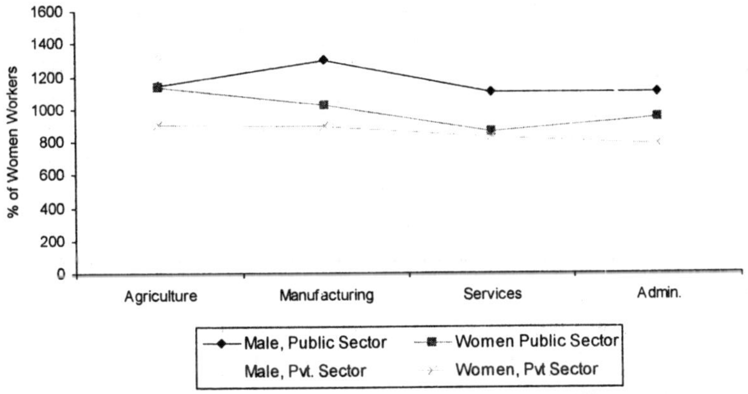

Figure 3.5: Wage Differentials by Sex in the Public and Private Secotrs.

Factors Affecting Employment of Women

Gender discrimination in employment and wages is well established, at least in developing countries including India. It is reflected in the size of women's employment and disparity in wages. Women are still a fraction of total employment in the formal as well as informal sectors in Indian economy. Agriculture claiming sizeable work force of women has inequality between male and female workers in terms of size and nature of employment and wages. In fact wage differentials are more pronounced in agricultural or rural sector than elsewhere. Even feminization of work seems to perpetuate inequality between men and women workers.

What are the factors that have caused women lagging behind men in the world of work? These impediments may be categorized, though over-lapping is not ruled out.

The list is, however, not exhaustive rather indicative and suggestive in nature. A general description is given below.

Religious Factors

Dogma

Religious scriptures intended to provide a way of life to the followers where women have been assigned more or less secondary role

CHART 3.1: Categories of Factors Affecting Women's Employment

Religious	Social	Economic	Biological	Psychological
Dogma	Attitude	Investment in Education	Reproduction	Sense of Insecurity
Segregation	Customs, Traditions	Training	Child Rearing	Lack of Confidence
	Domestic Chores	Low Payment	Physical	Inward Looking
	Marriage	Supplementing Income		Fear of Sexual Harassment
	Child Care	Lack of Unionism		
	Immobility	Inheritance		
	Dependency	Lack of Infrastructure		
	Accommodation			

in the society. They are directed and even commanded to follow men folk and hence women were deprived any role in decision-making. All this confined them within the four walls of the house and also discouraged women to be earners. Religious principles from which code of conduct emanated restricted the role of women in general and in economic sphere in particular. Sub-ordination of women is one of the command common in most religions.

Segregation

All religions generally preach segregation between spheres for men and women. It is one of the command for women to be home-maker. Their duties are to look after families, take care of children and remain confined to home. In fact women's reproductive role demarcates them from productive role of men. Such a social milieu commanded by religion leaves little room for the employment of women.

Indian society is still religious and largely believes in men-women inequality and, to some extent, segregation in the work sphere. Still women are mainly recognized for their reproductive functions and familial ties in the Indian society where religion holds an important place.

Social Factors

Attitude

Societal attitude is the most important factor and also responsible for low level of women's employment. Such an attitude which does not encourage women for employment has its roots in the patriarchy existing in the society since ages. It also relegated women to a secondary position and confined them to play the role of home-maker. Society in India does not favour employment of women as they are still looked upon as reproductive and not productive actors. Though matriarchical system prevails in some parts of India, especially in tribal belts, such examples may not be generalized to overrule patriarchy and hence men's dominance in the country at large. Working women is still an urban phenomenon due to changed attitude of urban society towards employment of women. The attitude of the society is changing mainly because of economic compulsions but has not changed enough to drastically affect the employment structure in the country.

Traditions, Customs and Taboo

Indian society value its traditions in the context of ancient civilization. Families still believe not to allow girls to work for income. And if they are allowed to work their income is not meant to run the house. Fathers are reluctant for their girls' employment in the first instance, and against utilizing their money for household expenses.

Customarily female children are discouraged to go out of town for education and particularly for employment. Again, economic compulsions are weakening such traditions and customs but not enough to mend societal attitude and make it positive for women's employment.

Certain occupations and jobs are considered favourably for women's employment. These are teaching, nursing and medical jobs. On the contrary a number of jobs are just like taboo in our society and women either discouraged or legally barred from such employment. For example taxi, truck or auto driving is not meant for women in India as these jobs are considered not safe. This protective umbrella rules out employment of women in a number of occupations and professions. Women are movers in the society but earth moving jobs are denied to them:

Domestic Chores

Since ancient time women's prime responsibility has been domestic chores as if they are meant for it. Any time-use survey of women would show that they have to spend considerable time performing domestic chores day after day. These have a wide range and mainly consisted of cooking, dish washing, laundary, house keeping and a host of other such activities. Even working women are not exempted from domestic chores.

It adversely affects their employment prospects. They have to do only those jobs which would give them enough time for domestic chores. Casualisation of women's employment is also because of their duty to perform domestic chores. Working women are not supposed to dispense with domestic chores and it seriously hampers their advancement. Those women who have nuclear family have to balance between domestic chores and job responsibilities. The same dilemma is faced by working women living with joint family. Women try to avoid those assignments in job which jeopardize their domestic activities and schedule. A compromise with their jobs due to unavoidable domestic chores affect their options in employment and promotions as well.

Marriage

In our society marriage seriously undermines employment of a female. Consequently she enters late in the job market or makes re-entry because they have to, sometimes, discontinue their employment on account of marriage. This particular custom has priority over every other thing and marriage comes first in case of females. The prime age, that is, around twenty-five is important for males to find employment but females are to marry at this juncture. Hence they loose employment opportunity in their prime age. Consequently women face the problem of re-entry or late entry into labour market. Therefore women's employment or prospects are compromised on account of marriage which is always on high agenda of every girl's parents.

Siblings/Child Care

Indian society has tradition of assigning responsibility, partially if not fully, to female children to look after young siblings in the family since female children are asked to take care of their young brothers and sisters, even in their childhood. Women have to devote a lot of time in taking care of their children as child care is taken as their sole responsibility in our society. Bearing and rearing children compells them to compromise with their employment. It acts as one of the main hurdles in the employment of women.

Immobility

Women have immobility in terms of space, time and energy. They are generally reluctant or have barriers to their movement from one place to another. It is either their own sense of insecurity or familial ties which bar their mobility in terms of space. Similarly their mobility in terms of time also gets affected during pregnancy and few months after delivery of baby. It makes them not very suitable for employment in those occupations requiring field work or traveling frequently. Hence immobility of women is considered an obstacle in their employment. Or they have to forego such jobs where mobility is a pre-requisite. It curtails their employment opportunities and options, and also acts as deterrent to their promotion in employment.

Dependency

The way female children are brought up in our society, especially in villages and towns that they become dependent on male persons. When they travel even as grown up, females depend on some male member of the family. It is observed that female applicants appearing for interview are usually accompanied by some family member. Such dependency discourages them to go for employment, particularly out of town. It makes them to remain confined to their place and hence restricts their employment opportunities and options. Dependency of women thus hinders their employment.

Accommodation

Women who get job or employment out of their town face the problem of accommodation from the point of view of safety and security. Those who are in employment and have transferable job find it difficult to move to far away places or rural area due to fear that they may not get a suitable accommodation. Therefore women workers try to avert this situation, sometimes at the cost of their employment. The problem of safe accommodation for women, especially working women is so grave that various committees have been formed to find a solution. Since working women hostels are extremely limited in number, women avoid such jobs where they have to move out from their town. Hence accommodation poses a big problem for working women and becomes a hindrance in employment, particularly out station employment in the interior places and rural area.

Economic Factors

Education

Investment in education gets priority for male children in Indian society. Female children rarely get preference in the matter of education especially at tertiary level. However returns to education in case of female education are high enough and make a strong case for education of girls. Parents usually compromise for the quality of education and expenses in case of female children as they invest just to educate them and not from the viewpoint of employment. On the contrary, male children's education primarily aims at their career and hence best possible education is provided to them. It is the reason for inequality in enrolment sex-ratio right from primary to tertiary level.

Training

Job-oriented courses of elementary nature are generally preferred for females rather than males. Women are largely in computer courses, boutique and fabric painting and similar elementary courses which lead them to low-paid jobs and land them in the secondary segment of labour market. Moreover, participation rate of women in training programmes to update knowledge and skills has been very low. Therefore, women's advancement in employment is generally hampered. Exclusive women training programmes are very few at least in the private sector. It partly explains the reason for women being largely in the low-paid jobs.

Unionism

Unionism is traditionally a male bastion and women have not registered significance in this regard. Women generally lack unionism as they have dual responsibility. Consequently women's unions are rare and as a member of common union they are occasionally active. In most of the organizations they are members as it is compulsive.

Lacking unionism among women workers make them relatively vulnerable and does not inspire to fight against sex based problems or odds. They rather depend on protective measures such as reservation in promotion and training programmes. As a result discrimination against women could not be eliminated in India.

Payment

Low payment offered to women has confined them to the lower cadre in employment. They usually accept discriminating wages and hence inequality has got perpetuated in rural and informal sectors. In small cities and towns women teachers, for example, get less remuneration than minimum wages paid to menial workers. Their own attitude is also responsible to some extent. They accept less remuneration rather than sitting idle at home. Wage differentials discourage them to go for performance and hence their career advancement gets blocked.

Supplementing Income

It is one of the objective of most females seeking employment. Societal attitude has inculcated in their minds that males are bread earners for the family and their role is secondary. Girls waiting for marriage work to supplement family income in large cases. This attitude is an obstacle for their career making. Similarly a large number of women particularly in the informal sector work to supplement family income.

Inheritance

Inheritance laws and traditions have made women more vulnerable in the matter of title to land and other assets. Customarily women do not inherit assets and property equal to their counterparts. Religion also plays a role in such law of inheritance. For example, Islamic laws entitle a female to inherit only half of male share in the family

Infrastructure

Lack of infrastructure and other facilities is hindrance in women's employment. Women have relatively negligible access to facilities, especially in the matter of credit. Even collateral rule does not accept women as guarantors unless they have fixed assets in their names. A discriminatory approach to provide infrastructural facilities to women is commonly observed in India. It also hampers their employment prospects.

Biological Factors

Women are discriminated against in employment on biological grounds. Jobs requiring physical strength are denied to them. Security jobs particularly in the private sector are restricted for women due to protective measures. Reproductive nature of women restrict their employment opportunities as it is presumed to increase the rate of labour turn-over.

It has been observed and studied that young women are

preferred in employment. Women beyond their prime age are discriminated against and those making re-entry find it difficult to get suitable employment. Age has become a deterrent for women above 40-45 age group as there are very few takers in the job market.

Child Rearing

Mothers with infants avoid employment as child rearing is considered their "natural" prime responsibility. Though the provision of crèches has been made mandatory, informal sector rarely provides such facilities to women workers with infants. Therefore child bearing and rearing are deterrent for women's employment.

Psychological Factors

Insecurity

Women feel insecure and avoid employment in such places where their security is not up to the mark. The poor law and order conditions aggravate their sense of insecurity. Consequently, working at not-so-familiar places and interior rural area is generally ruled out by them. In some cases feeling of insecurity is so strong that women prefer to remain home makers.

Confidence

Women's confidence for jobs other than considered suitable for them is not so strong and therefore they do not go for employment in a number of occupations like sales representative etc. They also lack confidence in case of employment requiring frequent travel by public transport. A majority of women is risk aversor by nature and avoid employment where risk element has high probability.

Inward Looking

Women born and brought up in traditional setting are generally inward looking and do not give much weight to employment. They prefer a settled married life. Hence a large number of women never try for employment and remain home makers. Inward looking attitude of Indian women, especially married women, deters them to go for employment. Their personal world revolve around their family.

Sexual Harassment Fear

Largely the fear of sexual harassment causes the fear of insecurity and lack of confidence among women. Sexual abuse, verbal and physical, always haunts in their mind, and guardians also feel uncomfortable, which daunts them to go for employment in those occupations and sectors considered not safe for women. Even women workers avoid those postings where they have apprehension of sexual abuse. Similarly night duty discourages them not only because of their family responsibility but also due to apprehension of sexual abuse.

Constitutional guarantee, ratification of the ILO Convention No. 100, and legal provisions have given protection to women workers but could not bring them at par with men. Professional attitude and consciousness for career has still not been inculcated among women in general and a majority of working women especially in low-paid jobs, in particular.

However, listing of various types of factors are indicative in nature and may be at variance in different cases. The plight of women in general and, working women in particular is well known in Indian society. There is a need of changing perception about women's work and its importance hither to neglected at political, social and economic levels in India.

REFERENCES

Arya, A. (2000), *Indian Women: Work and Development*, Gyan, Delhi, Vol. 3, pp. 199, 241, 317-18.

Labour Bureau (1998), Rural Labour Enquiry, 1993-94, Shimla.

Unni, J. (1999), "Women Workers in Agriculture: Some Recent Trends", in Papola, T.S. and Sharma, A.N. (Eds.), *Gender and Employment in India*, Vikas, Delhi, p. 105, Table 6.

Parthasarthy, G. and Nirmala, K. Annie (1999), "Marginalisation Hypothesis and Post Green Revolution Period" in Papola, T.S. and Sharma, A.N. (Eds.), *op. cit.*, p. 136.

Sharma, A. (1999), *Women and Work*, Gyan, Delhi, pp 22-24.

Chadha, G.K. (1999), "Non-Farm Employment in Rural Areas: How Well can Female Workers Compete?" in Papola, T.S. and Sharma, A.N. (Eds.), *op. cit.*, pp. 150-151.

Ministry of Labour, *Employment Review*, Govt. of India, various issues.

Jose, A.V. (1987), *Employment and Wages of Women Workers in Asian Countries*, ILO-ARTEP, Delhi.

Srivastava, N. (1999), "Striving for a Toe-hold: Women in the Organized sector" in Papola, T.S. and Sharma, A.N. (Eds.), *op. cit.*, p. 185.

Part Two

4

Women Workers in Eritrea

1. Background

4.0 *Introduction*

Woman employment in general and women's access to employment, in particular has gained importance as reflected by national legislations, NGO's concerned and working in this field, and efforts made by the ILO through its conventions and recommendations.

The International Labour Organization has made concerted efforts to promote gender equality and also status of women. Its Convention No. 100 resolved in 1951 focused on the equality of remuneration since women workers were paid less as compared with their male counterpart. Such efforts led to the principle, generally adopted by most of the countries, of equal work, equal remuneration and it got fortified through provisions in the national legislations. Women have always experienced discrimination not only in employment due to social, political, economic and religious reasons but also in the matter of occupations. Certain occupations were, and still are, not considered suitable for women and have been male bastions. It has been mainly on account of societal attitude towards women; lack of women's access to education, training, skill development and employment, lack of government policies and loop holes in legislations, sometimes labour laws which intended to protect women but were used to discriminate against them. Keeping in view such a socio-economic scenario, ILO's convention on discrimination in employment and occupation adopted in 1981 (Convention No. 111) made the member states to realize the need to eliminate discriminatory practices regarding women's employment and choice of occupation.

Another related aspect, which drew the attention of the ILO, has been workers with family responsibilities as reflected in the Convention No. 156 resolved in 1981.

ILO also provided a general framework for "strengthening the organization's capacity to appropriately meet the needs of its constituents (governments, employers and workers organizations)" through its Action Plan on Equal Opportunity and Treatment for Working Men and Women in 1987 (ILO, 1995, p. 77). The case of socio-economic progress of women has further been strengthened by the Arusha Strategies for Women's Advancement in 1984, Nairobi Forward-Looking Strategies in 1985 and Abuja Declaration on Participatory Development in 1990.

The ILO has also facilitated many studies on various aspects of women workers. Changing position of women in society traces tremendous changes in women's participation in the labour force. However, occupational segregation has been found as an obstacle in their development as it limits the opportunities available to women (ILO, 1983).

Similarly, status of women still presents a gloomy picture since little progress has been made in improving the position of women workers in the Third World including Africa and their participation in labour market has been insignificant (ILO, Dec. 1983).

Though women's participation in the labour force and productive employment have been considered the key to economic efficiency and growth at enterprise, national and international levels on the one hand, and to higher incomes and welfare at the household level on the other (ILO, 1994), but it is undermined due to several factor such as time, space and energy immobilities of women workers (ILO, 1983c).

Gender, work and population are interrelated issues which still suffer from the social shortcomings in terms of concept, methodology and analysis. Hence, women's activities, particularly in developing countries, could not be assessed in a proper manner. It means that methodological shortcomings have proved an obstacle in studying women workers' participation in productive activities (ILO, 1994d).

Another interrelated problem has been assessment of women's contribution to economic development which not only suffers from conceptual shortcomings but also methodological problems especially in identification and data collection (ILO. 1988).

The ILO, therefore, has rendered excellent service for studying and promoting women's participation in the labour market and set standards in this regard (ILO, 1991). However, the ILO forecasts indicate that the women's participation in the labour market shall come down from 15 million per year, during 1975-85, to 13 million per annum up to the year 2000 (ILO, 1995). It has perhaps been surmised upon the fall out of economic adjustment during 1980s.

What have been the main hurdles experienced in the gender equality vis-a-vis employment? Some of them may be listed as:

- Men's dominance in the world of work as a legacy;
- Societal attitude about women in general, and potential capability and family responsibilities of working women in particular;
- Occupational gender segmentation of women workers;
- Inadequate access to education, job, training and skill development;
- Women's immobility in terms of time, space and energy;
- Inadequate legislative provisions and implementation thereof, to protect the status of women equal to men; and
- Accounting system of GNP, not taking account of family labour as other forms of productive labour are accounted for it underestimates women's contribution in the national economy and hence undermines women workers at the periphery of remuneration system.

4.1 *Women's Development Concepts*

Various theories claim to support the cause of women development. In the 1950s, modernization theory advocated transition from traditional to modernised approach to solve the problem of backwardness. Its one of the surmises was that the benefits would percolate down to women and eventually lead to women's development. Hence, United Nations Economic Commission for Africa adopted the modernization theory with a view to ameliorate the socio-economic situation in Africa which would eventually promote women's socio-economic status.

However, the modernization theory could not bore the fruit as was expected and 1960s witnessed the prominence of Under-development theory, also known as Neo-Marxist theory. It gave rise to dependency theory accusing the international system for dependency of developing countries. The dynamic was conceived in a manner that dependency has been because of exogeneity of socio-economic forces and institutions.

The world and economies witnessed changes during the 1970s which gave birth to dependency reversal theories in the 1980s. The perception which emerged due to the approaches of adjustment, popularly termed as structural adjustment programmes (SAPs), was that the underdevelopment in developing countries has been due to their 'endogenous' factors and not because of exogeneity. A capitalistic approach was suggested as remedy calling for free market and private entrepreneur system for the advancement.

In the last decade of the Century, sustainable development and later on human development emerged as solution to save not only depleting resources for the posterity but also to have focus on human at the centre or development. It gained popularity and was accepted as one of the major goal of development in the world.

However, under currents began surfacing for women's development in various forms and hence, various concepts and approaches, keeping women at the centre emerged during this period.

4.2 *Women's Development Approaches*

The independence movements of the 1950s and 1960s gave rise to various concepts concerning women's development which were, of course, influenced by the development theory in one way or the other.

There has been a realization that women have very limited access to resources and their control over them which is detrimental to maximization of human well-being. How to tackle the problem? In this regard the following approaches to women's development may be identified.

4.2.1 *The Welfare Approach*

This approach has been based on distinction between reproductivity of women and productivity of men and hence women are recipient of benefits which percolate down due to development. Such a welfare notion had its roots in the modernization theory which influenced United Nations assistance in the 1960s and later on in the 1970s. It became an aspect of the basic needs programme.

It was an indirect approach to women's development where women were not at the centre but at the receiving end. This approach surmised that once development due to modernization takes place, it will lead to women's development as well. Hence, there was more emphasis on reducing global population rather than any concern for health and family responsibilities of women. However, revised strategy led to integration of women's health and family but still women were passive recipient and not at the centre stage of development.

The major flaw of the welfare approach was that it lacked a development perspective for women as it failed to recognise the productive role and socio-economic responsibilities of women. Moreover, welfare approach had dependency rather than self-reliance inherent in its notion as well as *modus-operandi* (Snyder and Tadesse, 1995)

4.2.2 *The Human Resource Development Approach*

As early as 1971 the human resource development approach was identified as a solution to the problem of women's development. It was, in fact, based upon the recognition of women's productivity and women were regarded as economic producers as well as community managers. And this recognition placed women at the centre stage for development. Such an approach was pioneered by the UN Economic Commission for Africa giving rise to women's programme in 1972 and which, in turn, led to the establishment of African Training and Research Centre for Women (ATRCW) in 1975.

Women's reproductive and productive roles got recognition

since the goal of development was set at 'creating better lives, with greater freedom and well-being for members of the family, the local community and the society as a whole' (ECA, 1971). The development component emanated from women's participation in liberation struggle in their countries and established their intention to participate in the governance of their country in the post-liberation period. The emergence of development goal was also accentuated as the emphasis has shifted from modernization to people's well-being (Snyder & Tadesse, p. 10).

The human resource development approach, a reversal of welfare approach in the sense that the former advocated for women's access to productive resources for development and hence aimed at women as direct beneficiary of development while the latter envisaged percolating down benefits of development to women.

The human resource development approach realized that women form more than half of human resources and development can not take place with out their participation and also their development. Therefore, women's access to education, technology, income meaning thereby gainful employment became inherent and essential elements of human resource development approach.

4.2.3 *Equity Approach*

Equality between men and women, in legal terms, gave rise to the equity approach to women's development. In fact, United Nations Commission on the Status of Women (CSW) had been concerned for the legal equality between the sexes and it led to the Convention on the Elimination of Discrimination Against Women (CEDAW).

The equity approach did not get preferential treatment or acceptance from the Economic Commission for Africa as there was apprehension that such legislation would not have impact on the status of women, especially for the majority of illiterate and rural women. It may also lead to confrontation about sexism and women find it better to provide for their children's well-being rather than confronting their men.

However, equity approach to women's development got recognition in the 1990s and the origin of the Commission on Human

Rights is traced back to Commission on the Status of Women. Africa is known for its human rights activities led by women (Snyder and Tadesse, pp. 11-12)

4.2.4 *The Anti-Poverty Approach*

The ILO and the World Bank's basis needs and absolute poverty theories promulgated and implemented in the 1970s experienced a shift in strategy to over come the hunger and malnutrition. This shift in the focus on poverty made women at the centre due to their family responsibilities.

It gave rise to income-generating and entrepreneurship projects to enable women to fulfil their family responsibilities, and hence women, despite limitations, got an access to formal financial institutions under the anti-poverty or poverty-alleviation programmes. Keeping in view the human resource development and poverty alleviation in the context of women's development, Economic Commission for Africa under its Women's Programme, designed its trainers' training programme for rural women constituting more than 80 per cent of all women in Africa (Snyder and Tadesse, p. 12).

4.2.5 *The Efficiency Approach*

Since women constitute more than half of the total population, their participation and development are bound to accelerate over all development. Hence the focus shifted from productivity to increasing productivity of women to raise the quality of life. Thus a need has been felt for development oriented approach leading to development and acceptance of the efficiency approach. However, apprehension has been that women's productivity may not increase if they don't have access to technological innovations (Boserup, 1970). But efficiency approach once becomes market-oriented, as it did, women's access to technology would be guided by the market.

In the late 1970s, structural adjustment programmes (SAPs) provided good basis for the criticism of the efficiency approach. It emphasized domestic adjustment and excluded the influence of global political, technological and economic factors. SAPs had bitter prescriptions, such as, severe cuts in government spending and reliance on free-market operation thus adversely affecting health and education system (Cornia et al., 1987) and leading to unemployment where the first victims would be women. Indeed, SAPs were expected to jeopardize gender planning with adverse implication for women's development (Moser, 1991).

In the scenario of structural adjustments, efficiency approach aiming at economic growth only, largely wiped gains made by women (Snyder and Tadesse, p. 13).

4.2.6 *The Empowerment Approach*

The mid-1980s witnessed the DAWN i.e. Development Alternatives with Women for a New era which championed the empowerment approach. It was emphatic in its approach for women's access to land, credit, education and training so as to enable women's self-reliance. It also advocated for entrusting autonomous women's organizations to ensure that targeted measures do reach women. Does it tantamount to women's empowerment through women? Certainly not, but there is a need to develop programme from women's perspectives (Sen and Grown, 1987). Hence, the approach emphasises women's participation for their self-reliance.

The discussion in the context of women's development in Africa may be concluded as:

> The ECA Women's Programme and the ATRCW pioneered the human resource development approach, which contained elements of the equity, efficiency, welfare, anti-poverty and empowerment approaches and both bodies practised gender analysis ... (Snyder & Tadesse, p. 15). At present, gender analysis has become not only a common parlance but also practice which received acceptance by the national and international agencies since the early 1990s.

4.3 *Definition*

The ILO has used the concept of employment following the

classical definition which "divides workers into four categories namely, the self-employed workers, employers, unremunerated family workers and remunerated family workers" (ILO, 1995, p. 77).

However, the categorisation stated above lacks in the respect that it does not take into account, *inter-alia*, apprentices. Moreover, drawing a distinction between self-employed and employers creates some problem as the former generally includes the latter especially in those economies where establishments are small. Hence, the present study has categorised women workers into (i) Salaried/Wage Labour (ii) Employers (iii) Family Labour and (iv) Apprentice. The operational definition is therefore, women engaged in economic activities and in return get remuneration are in 'employment'. It includes only gainful activities with remuneration and excludes all sorts of unremunerative activities from the purview of the term 'employment'.

Women's employment in Eritrea has been examined in terms of their participation in the non-agricultural activities, i.e. establishments, distribution of female labour force by industry, occupational distribution of women workers, and wage levels (Selassie, 1986).

4.4 *Objectives*

Main objective

The main objective has been to study the pattern of women employment in the establishments in Eritrea. However, specific objectives may be stated as:

Specific objectives

1. To measure the extent of women employment in Eritrean establishments;
2. To examine the pattern of women employment by industrial activity;
3. To investigate occupational distribution of women workers; and

4. Wage structure of women workers.

4.5 *Limitations*

However, the present study has, like any other, its own limitations. Firstly, collection of data done through the questionnaire method refers to single point of time. Secondly, data pertains to establishments only. Thirdly, the size of woman workers' sample has not been more than 1/3 of the total sample-size. Fourthly, sample is a part of survey of establishment carried out to assess the employment situation in general and not specifically for women workers. The present effort reflects exploration and not a comprehensive study since women's participation in total economy has not been the subject matter. Lastly, primary data have been collected for the present study as other sources are almost non-existent.

4.6 *Hypotheses*

In order to assess and investigate women's employment in Eritrea, the following hypotheses were formed:

(i) women are largely employed in the informal activities;
(ii) women workers are low paid as compared with male workers;
(iii) women in employment have less exposure to education and skills and; hence, are in the occupations with no future promotion;
(iv) women are in a disadvantageous situation *vis-a-vis* employment in terms of size, job-nature and job-relations;
(v) women are more prone to exploitation in employment than their male counterparts.

4.7 *Sum- up*

Gender issue has been in focus since early 1950s but not in the centre-stage till the 1990s. The conceptual development passed through various phases as reflected from the approaches to women's development. Consequently, gender problem got recognition particularly in the matter of income-generation and employment.

However, women employment in non-agricultural sector seems to be less in developing countries and a number of measures are still required to ameliorate the socio-economic situation of women, especially in Africa. In this regard, there is a need to assess the situation of women employment and formulate multi-pronged gender-based employment policy in Eritrea.

5

Over-View of Women Employment

5.0 Introduction

Gender issue in general and in terms of employment in particular has been given consideration by the Government. Macro-Policy providing guidelines for the socioeconomic development in Eritrea has laid down that:

(a) awareness would necessarily be created in the society about the decisive role of women for the socio-economic, political and cultural transformation of the country:
(b) women have equal rights and no discrimination on account of gender;
(c) efforts would be made to increase participation of women in education economic activities and employment;
(d) appropriate labour-saving technologies be promoted to reduce the drudgery of women in the household and other activities;
(e) mother-child care services will be improved and expanded.

(The Govt. of the State of Eritrea, 1994)

Therefore, gender-issue, particularly women's participation in employment has been taken care of. However, gender-balance in terms of employment may be analysed in the following manner.

5.1 Size of Women Employment

There are 22,139 establishments listed and these have a total employment of 98,293 workers with a male-female ratio of 67:33. Out of total establishments in the country a sample of 3,307 units was taken to assess the employment situation. Of the total workers, number of women workers turned out to 15,493, that is, around 34 per cent, thus affirming the ratio observed in the listing of establishments.

Since aggregate figures of employment fail to show the dispersion of women workers in various regions, a disaggregation at regional levels becomes important. The following table shows women workers' dispersion, and hence extent of variation, in various regions.

TABLE 5.1: Women Workers by Establishment and Zoba

Zoba	No. of Estab.	Per cent of Estab.	No. of women	Per cent of women	Per cent of total workers of region	Per cent of women in aggregate
Debubawi K.B.	139	4.2	502	3.2	27.6	1.1
Semeinawi K.B.	253	7.7	1,457	9.4	22.0	3.2
Anseba	400	12.1	859	5.5	29.6	1.9
Gash-Barka	389	11.8	511	3.3	27.6	1.1
Debub	452	13.7	1,235	8.0	28.7	2.7
Maekel	1,674	50.6	10,929	70.5	38.7	23.9
Total	3,307	100.0	15,493	100.0	33.9	33.9

Apparently relationship between units and women workers percentages seems to be weak. For example, Debubawi Zoba has 4.2 per cent of total units and employ 3.2 per cent of total women workers, but Gash-Barka Zoba which has 11.8 per cent of total units employs the same percentage of total women workers. In terms of total percentage, female workers are 27.6 per cent in Debubawi as well as in Gash Barka, Similarly Semeinawi shows the share of female workers as 22 per cent while it has 7.7 per cent total units.

In terms of total workers, percent share of women in all zobas other than Maekel has been extremely insignificant as it varies between 1.1 per cent and 3.5 per cent only. It is zoba Maekel which shows women's proportion in total employment around 24 per cent. Therefore, share of women workers in total employment around 34 per cent when distributed over various regions presents a dismal picture.

However, disaggregative analysis, that is, at regional level shows moderate participation of women workers varying between 22 and 38.7 per cent of total regional workers.

Dispersion of women workers in the region shows less variation but when their shares either in total females or total workers are depicted, fluctuations are heavily pronounced. Gender inequality in the matter of employment is visible in all the regions but less pronounced in the case of Zoba Maekel.

5.2 Employment-Nature of Women Workers

The nature of job, i.e. permanent or temporary is concerned with job security and thus future prospects of women workers. Data collection from establishment units shows shares of women workers as 35.8 per cent and 30.1 per cent in the permanent and temporary employment respectively. However, disaggregative situation at regional level may be seen from Table 5.2.

TABLE 5.2: Women Employment by Job-Nature

Zoba	Number of female workers in category of			
	Permanent	Per cent	Temporary	Per cent
Debubawi K.B.	281	27.2	221	28.1
Semeinawi K.B.	605	28.6	852	18.9
Anseba	578	29.2	281	29.1
Gash-Barka	402	25.9	109	36.5
Debub	953	31.3	282	22.4
Maekel	7,972	39.0	2,957	37.8
Total	10,791	35.8	4,702	30.1

The situation of women in both categories almost confirms pattern of total employment. However, permanent employment has a slight edge over temporary employment of women in the sense that the former shows higher percentage than the latter.

A striking feature at regional distribution has been that there are more percentages of temporary than permanently employment women in Gash-Barka and Debubawi. However, all other zobas show some what higher percentage of women in permanent employment category. Moreover, zoba Anseba shows an equal percentage of women workers in both the categories, while Semeinawi has the least i.e. 18.9 per cent of temporary women workers.

Hence, women workers are disadvantageously placed vis-a-vis male workers in permanent and temporary categories of employment. However, gender-inequality has been relatively higher in Gash-Barka followed by Debubawi zoba which have more percentage of female workers in temporary employment.

5.3 Women Workers by Job-Relations

The structure of employment determines the relative position of workers in the job market. It is recognized that larger the amount of family labour, dismal the future prospects. Conversely, larger the share as employer, better the future prospects of workers.

TABLE 5.3: Distribution of Women Workers by Job-Relations

Zoba	Salaried	Employer	Family worker	Apprentice	Total
Debubawi K.B.	436	37	29	–	502
	(86.9)	(7.4)	(5.8)	–	(3.2)
Semeinawi K.B.	1,343	55	40	19	1,457
	(92.2)	(3.8)	(2.7)	(1.3)	(9.4)
Anseba	713	91	54	1	859
	(83.0)	(10.6)	(6.3)	(0.1)	(5.5)
Gash-Barka	308	97	104	2	511
	(60.3)	(19.0)	(20.4)	(0.4)	(3.3)
Debub	970	154	109	2	1,235
	(78.5)	(12.5)	(8.8)	(0.2)	(8.0)
Maekel	10,134	417	359	19	10,929
	(92.7)	(3.8)	(3.3)	(0.2)	(70.5)
Total	13,904	851	695	43	15,493
	(89.7)	(5.5)	(4.5)	(0.3)	(100)

Note: Figures in parentheses show the per cent of row total Parentheses in total column show percentages of the column total.

Women workers by job-relations have been classified into: (i) Salaried Workers, (ii) Employers, (iii) Family Workers, and

(iv) Apprentices. The relative position of female workers may be assessed from their distribution in these categories.

The highest percentage has been found in Maekel for salaried workers (92.7 per cent). While Gash-Barka has the largest percentages for employers and family workers i.e. 19 per cent and 20.4 per cent respectively. And the share in apprentice category has been largest, among all the regions, in Zoba Semeinawi (1.3 per cent).

It is disappointing that the total number of female apprentice comes to only 0.3 per cent of total female workers. Salaried workers' overwhelming share i.e. 89.7 per cent of total women workers sampled shows that the relative position of female workers has been poor since wage earners' future prospects such as, higher income, promotion and career are usually not very promising. On the contrary, male workers distribution has been 58 per cent, 28 per cent and 14 per cent for salaried workers, employers and family workers respectively (MLHW, 2001). Thus women workers have more skewed distribution by job-relations than male workers in Eritrea. Moreover, skill development among women workers has been negligible since the share of apprentice comes to 0.3 per cent of their total. It also castes aspersion on the future prospects.

5.4 Age-Distribution of Women Workers

Demographic features affect the age distribution of workers in a country. Eritrea, just like any other African country has a large percentage of young population mainly due to population growth rate. Hence, it is bound to affect the age structure of workers.

Female workers' age distribution shows increasing percentage in the early age groups. Table 5.4 contains information collected from 3,307 units and 45,695 workers out of which female's number is 15,493.

It may be noted that the percentage of women in total workers increases from ≤ 19 to 25-29 age groups, and declines for 30-34 to 60 ≥ age group. However distribution of male workers total shows a contrary pattern that their percentage decreases from ≤ 19 to 25-99 age groups and rises from 30-34 and onwards. Age distribution of women workers show a declining percentage beyond 29 years and the fall is more rapid from 49 years and onwards.

TABLE 5.4: Age-Distribution of Women Workers

Age-group	No. of female workers	Per cent of total females	Per cent of grand total
≤ 19	1,986	12.8	36.6
20-24	2,232	14.4	40.6
25-29	2,779	17.9	41.7
30-34	1,961	12.1	41.3
35-39	1,969	12.7	39.6
40-44	1,771	11.4	38.7
45-49	1,394	9.0	30.5
50-54	881	5.7	23.5
55-59	309	2.0	11.9
60 ≥	211	1.4	7.3
Total	15,493	100.0	33.9

However distribution of male workers by age groups shows somewhat inverse of women's distribution.

Therefore, percentage shares of male and female workers in the total of respective age groups show a contrast. So the percentage share of males in total increases beyond 30-34 age group while declines for the women workers.

An interesting picture emerges when age groups are presented in terms of percentages of male and female workers in their respective totals. Female distribution increases till the age group of 25-29 years and then falls. But percentage of males in their total shows a peculiar pattern, i.e. decreasing and then increasing at every subsequent age-group interval.

Another important feature has been that around 54 per cent of total male workers fall in the age-range of 19 to 39 year, while it is around 71 per cent for women workers indicating that age distribution of women workers differs significantly. They are few in the higher age groups, especially beyond 50 years; while it is not so for the male workers.

5.5 Women workers by Nationality

It is reminded here that when information was being collected in

1999 Ethiopian workers were there as well. Since government policy was non-discriminatory, Ethiopians were significant in number in some regions and sectors. Hence, it is pertinent to study workers in terms of nationality as well.

Sampling of 3,307 units from all the regions had 45,695 workers, out of which 5,920, i.e. 13 per cent were Ethiopian workers. For analysis purpose, workers by nationality have been categorized into three viz. Eritrean, Ethiopian and others. Table 5.5 presents comparative statistics.

TABLE 5.5: Women Workers by Nationality

Zoba	Eritrean	Ethiopian	Others	Total
Debubawi	344 (68.5%)	156 (31.1%)	2 (0.4%)	502 (3.2%)
Semeinawi	1,128 (77.4%)	329 (22.6%)	–	1,457 (9.4%)
Anseba	727 (84.6%)	131 (15.3%)	–	859 (5.5%)
Gash-Barka	477 (93.3%)	33 (6.5%)	1 (0.1%)	511 (3.3%)
Maekel	1,084 (87.8%)	150 (12.1%)	1 (0.2%)	1,235 (8.0%)
Total	13,084 (84.5%)	2,394 (15.4%)	15 (0.1.%)	15,493 (100%)

Distribution of women workers shows that largest percentage of Eritreans has been in Gash-Barka zoba, i.e. 93.3 per cent of their total, while Ethiopian had it in zoba Debubawi, i.e. 31.1 per cent. Women workers of other nationality have been negligible.

However, out of total women workers Eritreans constitute 48.5 per cent, Ethiopians 15.4 per cent and others 0.1 per cent. It is interesting that the Ethiopian women workers have a larger percentage in their total than total Ethiopian workers have in the total labour force.

Another important feature emerges when shares of women workers are computed from their respective total. Eritrean women workers are 33.2 per cent of their total workers but Ethiopian women show a share of 40.4 per cent in their total. Therefore, participation rate of Ethiopian women workers in employment has been higher than that of Eritrean women workers. The following figure depicts the same.

Out of total sampled workers, i.e. 45,695 the share of Eritrean, Ethiopian and other women workers turned out to 28.6 per cent, 5.2 per cent and 0.03 per cent respectively. It clearly shows a poor participation rate of women workers in total employment.

5.6 Educational Level of Women Workers

Education's relevance to the world of work has been a debatable issue since the present educational system prepares students for the next level in general (Castley, 1986). In developing countries, education system in the post-liberalization era has started changing its orientation so as it is more relevant to the world of work. But mass education programme in Africa, due to heavy pressure of their society could not have a head away regarding re-orientation of educational system on any large scale.

Eritrea not only has a poor record of school enrolment and dropout due to socioeconomic compulsions but also a gender disparity which "widens enormously in rural areas at higher ages" (NSO, 1997). Moreover, lack of educational infrastructure and training institution has compounded the problem. School-leavers generally turn to the labour market and hence aggravate the problem of unemployment. Gender-disparity in education has further dampened the prospect of women employment in general and promotional avenues in particular. Such a scenario prompted to hypothesize that women workers must be less qualified and skilled and hence engaged in vocations requiring less or no education.

Table 5.6 presents distribution of women workers by educational levels.

Distribution of women workers by educational level shows maximum percentage of secondary educated followed by illiterate and primary educated women workers. In fact these three categories account for 94 per cent of total women workers meaning thereby only 6 per cent of them have education beyond the secondary level.

TABLE 5.6: Women Workers by Educational Level

Educational level	Number of women workers	Per cent	Number of total workers	Women as per cent of total workers
Illiterate	4,759	30.7	11,371	41.9
Primary	3,349	21.6	10,477	32.0
Secondary	6,766	43.7	20,660	32.8
Certificate	9	0.05	43	20.9
Diploma	289	1.9	1,273	22.7
University incomplete	182	1.2	926	19.7
First degree	130	0.8	826	15.7
Masters	7	0.04	86	8.1
Ph.D.	2	0.01	33	6.1
Total	15,493	100.0	45,695	33.9

But the distribution of women workers in terms of total labour presents even more depressing situation. Women are around 42 per cent of total illiterate workers followed by secondary (32.8 per cent) and primary educated (32 per cent).

If distribution of male and women workers are considered in the respective total by educational level than the following picture emerges.

A divergent pattern of distribution for male and female workers by the level of education may be observed. Hence a widening disparity exists between distribution of male and female workers by their educational level.

5.7 Sum-Up

The characteristics of women workers may be summed-up in the following manner.

(i) Women worker form one-third of total workers. Their share in total employment varies from zoba to zoba. However, zoba Maekel may claim for largest share of women workers as it employs 70.5 per cent of total women workers;

(ii) The share of women workers in the permanent category

of employment has been around 36 per cent while in the temporary employment percentage of women workers comes to around 30 per cent. Hence male dominance in both the categories of employment is obvious. There is only one region namely, Gash-Barka where percentage of temporary exceeds significantly than that of the permanent women workers;

(iii) Distribution of women workers at national level shows overwhelming dominance of salaried workers while their shares in the category of employer and family workers are insignificant;

(iv) Age-distribution of women workers shows a bias in favour of early age groups and against age groups beyond 30-34 years onwards. While distribution of male workers has been more fair than what it is for women workers;

(v) Workers have been categorized by their nationality into Eritrean, Ethiopian and Others. Eritrean women workers have been 84.5 per cent, of total while the shares of two other categories came to 15.4 per cent and 0.1 per cent respectively.

However, Eritrean women workers are around 33 per cent of their total workers while Ethiopians show a share of 40.4 per cent in their total number of workers. Hence, relative position of Ethiopians turned out better than Eritrean or women workers of other nationalities;

(vi) Analysis of women workers by educational level revealed an inverse relationship between the number of women workers and levels of education. Higher the level of education, lower the number of women workers. Moreover, men workers have an edge over women workers in terms of their share at every level of education. In fact percentage distribution curves for men and women workers by their educational level are almost divergent and thus show a wide disparity.

6

Sectoral Employment of Women

6.0 Introduction

Sectoral distribution reflects the structure of an economy and any structural change is, therefore, bound to affect sectoral structure as well. SAPs in Africa, inter-alia, led to the emergence and expansion of the informal sector (ILO, 1995). Such changes in the sectoral structure, in turn, have impact on labour absorption capacity. Informal sector has emerged as the major provider of employment. Therefore, employment and its growth largely depend upon the sectoral distribution and policies.

Eritrea follows international standard classification viz. ISCO-88 in the absence of national classification. Hence, sectoral distribution in Eritrea has eleven major industrial activities in accordance with the ISCO-88. Assessment of women employment thus be made in the context of industrial activities.

6.1 Women Employment and Industrial Activities

Distribution of women workers in various industrial activities has been given in Table 6.1(a). However, data contained in Table 6.1(a) pertain to 3,307 units falling in the sample.

There is only one sector namely, General Service where women worker out number male workers. In the rest of sectors, women's share in employment has been less than that of male workers.

Out of their total, distribution of women workers shows maximum percentage, i.e. 38.8 per cent in the Manufacturing sector

TABLE 6.1(a): Women Workers by Industrial Activities

Industrial activity	Total workers	Per cent	Total women workers	Per cent	Women as per cent of total workers
A. Agriculture, hunting and foresting	1,231	2.7	323	2.1	26.2
B. Fishing	6	–	3	–	50.0
C. Manufacturing	14,818	32.4	6,091	38.3	41.1
D. Mining and quarrying	185	0.4	30	0.2	16.2
E. Electricity, gas and water supply	3,128	6.8	317	2.0	10.1
F. Construction	8,715	19.1	1,585	10.2	18.2
G. General Trade	4,803	10.5	1,440	9.3	30.0
H. Transport, storage and communication	4,230	9.3	933	6.0	22.1
I. Finance and real estate renting	848	1.8	350	2.3	41.3
J. General Service	7,011	15.3	4,175	26.9	59.5
K. Professional Service	720	1.7	246	1.6	34.2
Total	45,695	100.0	15,493	100.0	33.9

Note: – negligible and hence omitted.

followed by the General Service (26.9 per cent). Comparing with the distribution of total male workers, women workers have their larger percentages in Manufacturing, General Service and, Finance and Real Estate Renting.

Distribution of men and women workers in their respective industrial activity total shows a similar pattern. Women worker's percentage distribution is generally less than that of men workers. However, women have significantly higher percentage of their total in Manufacturing and, Finance and Real Estate Renting sectors.

In aggregate, women have edge over male workers in General Service sector only. However, relative position of women workers in total employment may be seen from Table 6.1(b).

TABLE 6.1(b): Participation Level of Women Workers

Participation level	Per cent of grand total	Sectors	Rank*
Dominant i.e. ≤ 50%	59.5	General Service	I
	41.3	Finance and real estate renting	II
		Manufacturing	III
Significant	34.2	Professional service	IV
i.e. 25%-50%	30.2	General trade	V
	26.2	Agriculture, hunting and forestry	VI
Moderate	22.1	Transport, storage and communication	VII
i.e. ≤ 25%	18.2	Construction	VIII
	16.2	Mining and quarrying	IX
	10.1	Electricity, gas and water supply	X

6.2 Women Employment and Job-Nature

Job-nature indicates job-security and also signifies promotional and other benefits. Therefore, women workers have been classified into permanent and temporary in employment and studied accordingly. Table 6.2(a) shows distribution of women workers in various sectors by the nature of job.

Women's share in total permanent employment has been around 36 per cent. Out of total women workers, largest percentage i.e. 44.4 per cent has been absorbed in the Manufacturing

TABLE 6.2(a): Women Employment (Permanent) by Job-Nature

Industrial activity	Number	Per cent	Per cent share in sector	Total permanent workers	Per cent of total permanent workers
A. Agriculture, hunting and forestry	143	1.3	20.5	699	0.5
B. Fishing	3	–	–	6	–
C. Manufacturing	4,792	44.4	41.9	11,444	15.9
D. Mining and quarrying	23	0.2	15.9	145	0.1
E. Electricity, gas and water supply	109	1.0	11.8	925	0.4
F. Concentration	538	5.0	16.6	3,248	1.8
G. General trade	979	9.1	26.9	3,638	3.3
H. Transport, storage and communication	881	8.2	23.5	3,751	2.9
I. Finance and real estate renting	286	2.7	39.0	734	0.9
J. General service	2,821	26.1	56.9	4,954	9.4
K. Professional service	216	2.0	40.4	534	0.7
Total	10,791	100.0	35.9	30,078	35.9

TABLE 6.2(b): Women Employment (Temporary) by Job-Nature

Industrial activity	Number	Per cent	Per cent share in sector	Total temporary workers	Per cent of total temporary workers
A. Agriculture, hunting and forestry	180	3.8	33.8	532	3.4
B. Fishing	–	–	–	–	–
C. Manufacturing	1,299	27.6	38.5	3,374	21.6
D. Mining and quarrying	7	0.1	17.5	40	0.3
E. Electricity, gas and water supply	208	4.4	9.4	2,203	14.1
F. Concentration	1,047	22.3	19.2	5,467	35.0
G. General trade	461	9.8	39.6	1,165	7.4
H. Transport, storage and communication	52	1.1	10.9	479	3.1
I. Finance and real estate renting	64	1.4	56.1	114	0.7
J. General service	1,354	28.8	65.8	2,057	13.2
K. Professional service	30	0.6	16.1	186	1.2
Total	4,702	100.0	30.1	15,617	30.1

sector followed by General Service Sector (26.1 per cent). All other industrial activities have a share of less than 10 per cent of total women workers.

When the share of women workers is calculated in the individual industrial activity, then the General Service sector emerges as the major employer, closely followed by the Manufacturing, Professional Service, and Finance and Real Estate Renting sectors.

However, distribution of women workers by industrial activity in total permanent employment shows the Manufacturing sector has largest share, i.e. followed by General Service (9.4 per cent). All other industrial activities show very insignificant proportion of women workers in total permanent employment.

The percentage of temporary workers in total comes to 30.1 per cent meaning thereby that male workers have a dominance even in temporary employment. When the shares of temporary workers in total temporary employment is worked out, Construction sector shows largest, i.e. 35 percentage followed by the Manufacturing (21.6 per cent) and, Electricity, Gas and Water Supply (14.1 per cent) sectors.

There are more violent fluctuations for temporary as compared with the permanently employed workers. It is particularly wild for the Construction sector where women workers are only 1.8 per cent of total permanent workers but 35 per cent of total temporary workers. In fact the range of disparity is largest between distance D-G covering Mining and Quarrying; Electricity, Gas and Water Supply; Construction and; General Trade. However, maximum disparity has been found in case of Construction sector.

6.3 Women Workers and Job-Relations

The relative position of women workers may be determined by analysing their shares in the categories of salaried workers, employers and family workers. Table 6.3 shows distribution of women workers by job-relations.

Family labour accounts for 40.2 per cent while salaried workers and employers have a share of 34.2 per cent and 30.7 per cent in the total of the respective categories. While the shares of women workers, falling in the categories, in total employment come to 89.7

TABLE 6.3: Women Workers by Industrial Activity and Job-Relations

	Total	Women	Per cent of total	Total	Women	Per cent of total	Total	Women	Per cent of total
Agriculture, hunting and forestry	1,093	314	28.7	103	7	6.8	35	2	5.7
Fishing*	6	3	–	–	–	–	–	–	–
Manufacturing	13,559	5,868	43.3	611	114	18.7	334	97	29.0
Mining and quarrying	180	30	16.7	4	–	–	1	–	–
Electricity, gas and water supply	3,126	317	10.1	–	–	–	2	–	–
Construction	8,626	1,582	18.2	65	2	3.1	16	1	6.3
General trade	3,361	1,079	32.2	726	180	24.8	509	176	34.9
Transport, storage and communication	4,212	932	22.1	5	–	–	1	1	–**
Finance and real estate renting	844	349	41.4	3	–	–	1	1	–**
General service	4,459	3,208	64.7	1,200	539	44.9	809	402	50.0
Professional service	642	222	34.6	51	9	17.6	24	15	62.5
Total	40,608	13,904	34.2	2,768	851	30.7	1,727	695	40.2

*Omitted from the analysis due to inappropriate sample.

**Inappropriate.

per cent, 5.5 per cent, 4.5 per cent and 0.3 per cent respectively. However, these shares in total employment fail to show distribution of women workers by industrial activities and corresponding job-relation.

Table 4.3 shows that women workers are non-existent in certain sectors under employers, and family workers categories. Other extreme is that women workers under the head of family workers are 100 per cent in some other sectors. Hence distribution is more skewed in case of women family workers, followed by women employers.

6.4 Woman Workers and Age-Distribution

Theoretically, age distribution in employment should be in consonance with demographic pattern, of course barring under-age workers and under-age population both. However, employment distribution is rarely in conformity with natural distribution of population. Distribution of women in employment differs form that of male workers especially in the Third World due to societal structure and attitude. The following analysis is to examine age-distribution of women workers and also to evaluate it in the context of age distribution of male workers so as to bring disparities to be taken care of.

Table 6.4 presents age-distribution of women workers in various industrial activities.

Age-distribution of women workers by industrial activity shows that ≤ 19, 20-24 and 60 ≥ age-groups have their largest shares in the General Service Sector, while the rest of age groups have largest percentage distribution of women workers by age and industrial activity. It is clear from Table 6.4 that women workers in relatively young age groups, say, ≤ 19 and 20-24 years are largely concentrated in the General Service Sector while the Manufacturing sector has the largest percentage of total women workers of higher age groups.

6.5 Women Workers by Nationality and Industrial Activity

Keeping in view the employment by nationality, women workers

TABLE 6.4: Age-Distribution of Women Workers by Industrial Activity

Age-group	Industrial activity											
	A	B	C	D	E	F	G	H	I	J	K	Total
≤ 19	129	–	406	–	15	193	250	8	1	974	10	1,986
%	(6.5)	–	(20.4)	–	(0.8)	(9.7)	(12.6)	(0.4)	(0.05)	(49.0)	(0.5)	(100.0)
20-24	40	–	507	2	75	343	214	67	32	910	42	2,232
%	(1.8)	–	(22.7)	(0.1)	(3.4)	(15.4)	(9.6)	(3.0)	(1.4)	(40.8)	(1.9)	(14.0)
25-29	57	2	802	6	78	447	236	270	95	715	71	2,779
%	(2.1)	–	(28.9)	(0.2)	(2.8)	(16.1)	(8.5)	(9.7)	(3.4)	(25.7)	(2.6)	(100.0)
30-34	32	–	788	4	31	206	154	212	66	429	39	1,961
%	(1.6)	–	(40.2)	(0.2)	(1.6)	(10.5)	(7.9)	(10.8)	(3.4)	(21.9)	(2.0)	(100.0)
35-39	19	1	926	10	50	162	156	165	72	378	30	1,969
%	(1.0)	–	(47.0)	(0.5)	(2.5)	(8.2)	(7.9)	(8.4)	(3.7)	(19.2)	(1.5)	(100.0)
40-44	20	–	973	3	33	109	159	112	42	288	32	1,771
%	(1.1)	–	(54.9)	(0.2)	(1.9)	(6.2)	(9.0)	(6.3)	(2.4)	(16.3)	(1.8)	(100.0)
45-49	14	–	876	4	18	77	101	35	22	235	12	1,394
%	(1.0)	–	(62.8)	(0.3)	(1.3)	(5.5)	(7.2)	(2.5)	(1.6)	(16.9)	(0.9)	(100.0)
50-54	7	–	584	1	9	25	75	49	17	109	5	881
%	(0.8)	–	(66.3)	(0.1)	(1.0)	(2.8)	(8.5)	(5.6)	(1.9)	(12.4)	(0.6)	(100.0)
55-59	2	–	170	–	6	11	41	13	2	61	3	309
%	(0.6)	–	(55.0)	–	(1.9)	(3.6)	(13.3)	(4.2)	(0.6)	(19.7)	(1.0)	(100.0)
60 ≥	3	–	59	–	2	12	54	2	1	76	2	211
%	(1.4)	–	(28.0)	–	(0.9)	(5.7)	(25.6)	(0.9)	(0.5)	(36.0)	(0.9)	(100.0)
Total	303	3	6,091	30	317	1,585	1,440	933	350	4,175	246	15,493
%	(2.1)	–	(39.3)	(0.2)	(2.0)	(10.2)	(9.3)	(6.0)	(2.3)	(26.9)	(1.6)	(100.0)

may largely be classified into Eritrean, Ethiopian and Others. Table 4.5 presents distribution of women workers in various sectors by their nationality.

Eritrean women workers constitute 84.5 per cent while Ethiopian only 15.4 per cent of the total. Women workers of other nationalities are negligible.

Out of Eritrean total women workers, 42.1 per cent are employed in the Manufacturing sector followed by General Service sector (20.2 per cent). But the Ethiopian women workers had their concentration (64 per cent) in the General Service followed by Manufacturing sector. Sectors other than these have insignificant proportion of women workers.

Women workers of other nationalities have their largest percentage in the Professional Services (33.3 per cent) followed by Manufacturing and the General Service sectors (20 per cent each).

Various sectors, e.g., Mining and Quarrying; Electricity Gas and Water Supply; Professional Services have very insignificant participation level of women workers since their number or percentage of total has been negligible. Hence, women are under represented in many sectors of the economy.

In every sector, Eritrean women have overwhelming majority since average percentage comes to around 92 per cent while it is around 8 per cent for the Ethiopian women workers. It is interesting to note that the Eritrean women workers' have largest concentration in the Transport, Storage and Communication sector (99.1 per cent) followed by Agriculture, Hunting and Forestry sector (97.8 per cent), if sector-wise total are considered.

6.6 Women Workers by Educational Level and Industrial Activity

The surmise has been that women have less qualification and skills in every sector in absolute and relative terms. Societal attitude towards female education has gone through a positive change due to efforts made by international organizations, NGOs and governments concerned. However, social transformation has not been fast enough due to the enormity of the educational problem of females.

The present study has selected education as one of the key

TABLE 6.5: Women Workers by Nationality and Industrial Activity

Industrial activity	Eritrean	Per cent	Ethiopian	Per cent	Others	Per cent	Total
Agri., Hunting & Forestry	316	2.4	7	0.3	–	–	323
	(97.8)	–	(2.2)	–	–	–	
Fishing	3	–	–	–	–	–	3
	–	–	–	–	3	–	
Manufacturing	5,503	42.1	585	24.4	(0.1)	20.0	6,091
	(90.3)		(9.6)	–	1	–	
Mining & Quarrying	29	0.2	–	–	(3.3)	6.7	30
	(96.7)		–	–	–	–	
Elec., Gas & Water Supply	304	2.3	13	0.5	–	–	317
	(95.9)		(4.1)	–	–	–	
Construction	1,508	11.5	75	3.1	2	13.3	1,585
	(95.1)		(4.7)	–	(0.2)	–	
General Trade	1,284	9.8	155	6.5	1	6.7	1,440
	(89.1)		(10.7)	–	–	–	
Trans., Storage & Comm.	925	7.1	8	0.3	–	–	933
	(99.1)		(0.9)	–	–	–	
Fin. & Real Est. Renting	339	2.6	11	0.5	–	–	350
	(96.9)		(3.1)	–	3	–	
General Service	2,640	20.2	1,532	65.0	(0.1)	20.0	4,175
	(63.2)		(36.7)	–	–	–	
Professional Service	233	1.8	8	0.3	5	33.3	246
	(94.7)		(3.3)	–	(2.0)	–	
Total	13,084	100.0	2,394	100.0	15	100.0	15,493
	(84.5)		(15.4)	–	(0.1)		

Note: Figures in parentheses show per cent of row total.

variable for data collection and analysis. Table 4.6 shows distribution of women workers by educational level, The present study has selected education as one of the key variable for date collection in various industrial activities. However, a poor relationship between the number of distributed in various industrial activities and educational level is also an indicator of the poor relevance of education for the world of work.

Agriculture and Manufacturing sectors show illiterates as largest percentage of their total. Otherwise workers with primary and secondary education dominate in most of the sectors.

Illiterate and primary educated women workers have largest percentage in the Agriculture, Hunting and forestry sector, while secondary educated women workers show their highest percentage in the Transport, Storage and Communication sector. University drop out, Graduates and Doctorate holding women workers are maximum in percentage in the Professional Service sector. While women workers with Masters are maximum in the Mining and Quarrying sector.

In aggregate, women workers in the illiterate category account for 30.7 per cent of their total number. This percentage has been higher when compared with male workers, i.e. 24.9 per cent of total male workers.

6.7 Sum-Up

Sectoral distribution of women workers may be summed-up as follows:

- Women workers have concentration in the Manufacturing sector where they constitute around 39 per cent of their total. But their percentage share, if taken in the total of individual sector, has been largest in the case of the General Service sector. Intact women out number male workers, being 59.5 per cent of total workers in the General Service sector.
- Women have a share of around 36 per cent in the permanent employment and 30 per cent in temporary employment. Therefore, women workers lag behind in employment as

TABLE 6.6: Women Workers by Educational Level & Industrial Activity

No.	Industrial activity	Illi.	Prim.	Sec.	Cert.*	Dip.*	Deg.	Mas.	Ph.D.	Total
A.	Agriculture, hunting and forestry	156	134	30	–	–	1	2	–	323
B.	Fishing*	–	2	1	–	–	–	–	–	3
C.	Manufacturing	2,417	1,765	1,768	1	94	19	26	1	6,091
D.	Mining and quarrying	8	6	10	–	3	1	1	1	30
E.	Electricity, gas and water supply	62	62	144	–	28	9	11	–	317
F.	Construction	441	594	507	–	17	19	6	1	1,585
G.	General trade	327	359	675	–	33	27	19	–	1,440
H.	Transport, storage and communication	43	137	665	7	32	34	13	2	933
I.	Finance and real estate	16	34	196	–	64	16	24	–	350
J.	General service	1,276	1,392	1,463	–	4	27	13	–	4,175
K.	Professional service	13	33	138	1	14	29	15	2	246
	Total	4,759	4,518	5,597	9	289	182	130	7	15,493

Note: *shows insignificant no. or per cent and hence omitted from the analysis.

compared to male workers, by the nature of job;

- Classification of women workers by job-relations gives relative shares of women, In total employment, salaried women workers are 30.8 per cent, employers 1.9 per cent and family labour accounts for 1.5 per cent. However, these shares in category total come to 34.2 per cent, 30.7 per cent, and 40.2 per cent respectively. This is a completely different picture presented by these figures;
- Age-distribution by industrial activity shows concentration of women workers in the age-range of 19 to 24 years in the Manufacturing sector, while other and higher age groups are largely concentrated in the General Service sector;
- Distribution of women workers shows that Eritreans have an edge over the Ethiopians as far as the total number of women workers is concerned, but latter have edge over the former in the matter of proportion in their total. Moreover, Eritrean women workers have largest percentage of their total in the Manufacturing sector, while Ethiopians have their concentrations in the General Service sector.

  Certain sectors like Mining and Quarrying; Electricity, Gas and Water Supply show negligible number of women workers of any nationality.
- The percentage of illiterate women workers dominates in the Agricultural and, Manufacturing sectors. School-leavers generally dominate in all other sectors. Secondary educated women workers are by and large, maximum in total as well as in different sectors.

However, ratio of illiterate women workers has been more than that of the male workers in the country. Moreover, less educated are more in employment than those educated beyond secondary level. And it is true for women and men both employed in the establishments covered by the Survey.

7

Occupational Distribution of Women Workers

7.0 Introduction

Occupational sex segregation has been a major issue especially in developing countries. Societal structure imbibing a host of socio-economic factors leads to occupational segregation by sex. Modernization has, to some extent, lowered down the barriers for females in various occupations. Otherwise traditional societies had, and still have, occupational segregation of one or the other kind for females in various countries. However, access to technology and education have led females even in those occupational areas considered as male bastions.

7.1 Women Workers by Occupation

First indicator of occupational segregation or integration may be the participation level of women in various occupations in the country. Therefore, statistics of women workers to assess women's participation by occupational categories and analysis assume importance *per se.* Following table contains information regarding the number of women workers by occupational categories.

Women Workers have dominating share in two occupational categories viz. Service, Shop and Market Sales Workers, and Clerks. They have over one-third share in the categories of Technicians and Associate Professionals, Elementary Occupations and Plant-Machine Operators and Assemblers. While women workers

TABLE 7.1(a): Women Workers by Occupational Categories

Occupation	No. of women workers	Per cent	No. of total workers	Per cent	Women workers as per cent of total workers
A. Legislators, senior officials and managers	1,076	6.9	4,311	0.4	25.0
B. Professionals	475	3.0	1,958	4.3	24.3
C. Technicians and Asso. Professionals	483	3.1	1,207	2.6	40.0
D. Clerks	2,033	13.1	3,775	8.3	53.9
E. Service, Shop and Mkt. Sales Workers	2,340	15.1	4,057	8.9	57.4
F. Skilled Agri. and Fishery Workers	16	0.1	192	0.4	8.3
G. Crafts and Related Trades	1,870	12.1	10,896	23.8	17.2
H. Plant, Machine Operators and Assemblers	2,259	14.6	6,186	13.5	36.5
I. Elementary Occupations	4,941	31.9	13,113	28.7	37.7
Total	15,493	100.0	45,695	100.0	33.9

represent around one-fourth in the categories of Legislators, Senior Officials and Managers; and Professionals.

The pattern of occupational distribution of women, men and total workers are of the same nature. The only difference has been in the extent of fluctuations which differ from each other, particularly for men and women workers.

Women have an edge over male distribution particularly in the categories of Technicians and Associate Professionals; Clerks and Service, Shop and Market Sales Workers. While male workers have edge over women workers in many categories, especially Legislators, Senior Officials and Managers; Craft and Related Trades.

Moreover, there is positive correlation between women workers and total workers by occupational categories since r = 0.707. It means women workers have a high degree of correlation vis-a-vis total workers by occupational categories.

In order to estimate the extent of occupational segregation by sex, a popular measure, i.e. Dissimilarity index, D, has generally been used (Jacobs and Lim, 1995). "It expresents the proportion of women who would have to change occupations for women to be distributed in the same manner as men" (Jacob and Lim, p. 273). The following table shows results with respect to occupational segregation by sex in Eritrea.

Dissimilarity index D for Eritrea shows a value of 49.999 = 50 per cent meaning thereby that occupational sex segregation has been moderate in Eritrea. It is even less than what many developed countries, e.g. USA had i.e. 57.3 per cent in 1986. Eritrea thus moving towards declining occupational sex segregation, but such an inference may be confirmed if statistics on women employment is regularly collected and subjected to analysis.

7.2 Women Workers by Job Nature and Occupation

Distribution of women workers by job-nature helps in understanding not only their participation in employment but also the security of job available to them. The maximum percentage of permanent women workers has been in the Service, Shop and Market Sales' occupational category (56 per cent) followed by Clerks (53

TABLE 7.1(b): Dissimilarity Index of Occupational Sex Segregation

Occupational Category	Di	D
Legislators, Senior Officials and Managers	D_1	5.356
Professionals	D_2	2.455
Technicians and Associate Professionals	D_3	1.199
Clerks	D_4	2.884
Service, shop and Market Sales Workers	D_5	2.843
Skilled Agricultural and Fishery Workers	D_6	.291
Craft and Related Trade Workers	D_7	14.943
Plant and Machine Operators and Assemblers	D_8	6.501
Elementary Occupations	D_9	13.527
Total	$\sum_{i=1}^{9} Di$	49.999

Jacobs, Jerry A. and Lim Suet T. (1995), "Trends in Occupational and Industrial Sex Segregation in 56 Countries, 1960-1980" in Jacob, Jerry (ed.), *Gender Inequality at Work*, California, Sage, pp. 259-293.

per cent). In all other occupational categories, their percentage varies between 10 per cent and 42 per cent as may be seen from Table 7.2.

As temporary employee, women have large percentage in the categories of Service, Shop and Market Sales (61.2 per cent) and Clerks (60.2 per cent). Surprisingly, these are occupation in which women also have largest percentage as permanent employee.

In order to find out whether any relationship exists between permanent women employees and total employees on the one hand, and temporary women workers and total workers on the other, coefficients of correlation have been estimated. Women workers in permanent-employment show a weak relation with total workers as the correlation coefficient worked out to 0.278. However, correlation between temporary women workers and temporary total workers turned out to 0.889, showing a very strong and positive correlation. Therefore, women in temporary jobs are worst off as compared to their position in the permanent jobs. Moreover, a strong correlation has also been found between permanent and temporary women workers since the coefficient of correlation comes to 0.723. It indicates a strong possibility of

TABLE 7.2 Women Employment by Occupation and job Nature

Occupation	Permanent				Temporary			
	Women	Per cent	Total	Women as per cent of total	Women	Per cent	Total	Women as per cent of total
A. Legislators, Senior Officials and Managers Professionals	1,052	9.7	4,182	25.1	24	0.5	129	18.6
B. Professionals	437	4.1	1,680	26.0	38	0.8	278	13.7
C. Technicians and Professionals	448	4.2	1,065	42.1	35	0.7	142	24.6
D. Clerks	1,728	16.0	3,268	52.9	305	6.5	507	60.2
E. Service, Shop and Mkt. Sales	1,530	14.2	2,734	56.0	810	17.2	1,323	61.2
F. Skilled Agri. and Fishery Workers	15	0.1	148	10.1	1	0.02	44	2.3
G. Craft and Related Trades	1,395	12.9	6,272	22.2	475	10.1	4,624	10.3
H. Plant-Machine Oper. and Assem.	1,857	17.2	5,123	36.2	402	8.5	1,063	37.8
I. Elementary Occupations	2,329	21.6	5606	41.5	2612	55.6	7,507	34.8
Total	10,791	100.0	30,078	36.0	4,702	100.0	15,617	30.1

increasing employment of women in either category due to an increase in any type of women employment.

7.3 Women Workers by Job Relations

The relative place of women in employment and their economic empowerment as well may be assessed from their employment distribution by job-relations. The surmise here is that if women workers are more in the employers category, they are better placed. On the contrary, if women workers have larger share in family labour, they have poor placement in the labour market and are economically worst off. Table 7.3 shows their distribution by job-relations.

Salaried women workers are maximum of their total in the Elementary Occupations followed by Plant-Machine Operators and Assemblers; Service, Shop and Market Sales and Clerks etc., confirming, to some extent, distribution of total workers. In the employers category, women workers are largely concentrated (76.3 per cent) in the Legislators, Senior Officials and Managers and rest of occupational categories have nominal percentage of their total. While family workers' category shows largest percentage, i.e. around 42 per cent in the occupational category of Service, Shop and Market Sales, followed by Clerks (22.4 per cent) and Legislators, Senior Officials and Managers (20.4 per cent). Women apprentice are largely found in the Craft and Related Trades; Legislators, Senior Officials and Managers and Service, Shop and Market Sales.

Women workers have higher percentage of their total than that of total workers in certain occupations like Clerks; Service, Shop and Market Sales and Elementary Occupations in all the three categories viz. salaried workers, employers, and family workers. However, women apprentices have larger than total worker's percentage in the occupational category of Legislators, Senior Officials and Managers.

7.4 Women Workers by Occupation and Age

Skewed age-distribution of employed women is a general observation, as stated elsewhere. In this section, however, age-distribution

TABLE 7.3 Women Workers by Occupation and Job-Relation

Occupation	Salaried women workers	Total workers	Employer women workers	Total workers	Family women workers	Total workers	Appr. women workers	Total workers
A. Legislators, Sr. Officials and Managers	272 (2.0)	1,683 (4.1)	649 (76.3)	2,175 (78.6)	142 (20.4)	433 (25.1)	13 (30.2)	20 (3.4)
B. Professionals	454 (3.3)	1,881 (4.6)	8 (0.9)	48 (1.7)	13 (1.9)	28 (1.6)	– –	1 –
C. Technicians and Asso. Profes.	459 (3.3)	1,124 (2.8)	10 (1.2)	45 (1.6)	12 (1.7)	29 (1.7)	2 (4.7)	9 (1.5)
D. Clerks	1,806 (13.0)	3,384 (8.3)	69 (8.1)	111 (4.0)	156 (22.4)	269 (15.6)	2 (4.7)	10 (1.7)
E. Service, Shop and Mkt. Sales	1,959 (14.1)	3,342 (8.2)	81 (9.5)	146 (5.3)	291 (41.9)	554 (32.1)	9 (20.9)	15 (2.6)
F. Skilled Agri. and Fishery Workers	16 (0.1)	188 (0.5)	– –	–	– –	4 –	– –	– –
G. Craft and Related Trades	1,812 (13.0)	9,928 (24.4)	17 (2.0)	194 (7.0)	27 (3.9)	291 (16.9)	14 (32.6)	480 (81.6)
H. Plant-Machine Oper. and Assem.	2,240 (16.1)	6,105 (15.0)	4 (0.5)	16 (0.6)	13 (1.9)	32 (1.9)	2 (4.7)	33 (5.6)
I. Elementary Occupations	4,886 (35.1)	12,973 (31.9)	13 (15)	33 (1.2)	41 (5.9)	87 (5.0)	1 (2.3)	20 (3.4)
Total	13,904 (100.0)	40,608 (100.0)	851 (100.0)	2,768 (100.0)	695 (100.0)	1,727 (100.0)	43 (100.0)	588 (100.0)

Note: Figure in parenthesis show per cent in total

of women workers by occupation has been analyzed. Table 7.4 shows distribution of women workers in different occupational categories by age-groups.

TABLE 7.4: Distribution of Women Workers by Occupation and Age

Age-group	No. of women workers by occupation								
	A	B	C	D	E	F	G	H	I
≤ 19	21	4	20	136	655	1	121	200	826
20-24	55	36	41	338	600	3	217	213	729
25-29	114	106	109	523	464	4	333	269	857
30-34	133	105	85	365	212	2	238	289	532
35-39	158	114	88	309	180	1	272	255	592
40-44	172	69	63	206	101	1	287	346	526
45-49	156	28	30	90	68	1	220	353	448
50-54	120	8	34	47	28	2	133	268	241
55-59	64	5	9	10	20	-	34	58	109
60 ≥	83	-	4	9	12	1	15	8	79
Total	1,076	475	483	2,033	2,340	16	1,870	2,259	4,941

Elementary Occupations show largest number of women workers of every age group, except 50-54 which has largest number in the Plant-Machine Operators and Assemblers category and 60 years and above have largest number in Legislators, Senior Officials and Managers' category.

Individually, Legislators, Officials and Managers' occupational category has maximum number of women workers in the age-group of 40-44, and Professionals in 35-39 age group, while Technicians and Associate Professionals; Clerks; Skilled Agricultural and Fishery Workers; Craft and Related Trades and Elementary Occupations show their largest number of women workers in 25-29 age groups. The remaining occupations, such as, Service, Shop and Market Sales, and Plant- Machine Operators and Assemblers show largest number of women workers of their respective total in the age-groups of 219 and 45-49 years respectively.

7.5 Women Workers by Occupation and Nationality

Women workers in Eritrea have been, on the basis of nationality, divided into three categories: Eritrean, Ethiopian and Others. Their distribution by occupation has been given in Table 7.5.

Eritrean women have largest percentage of their total in the Elementary Occupations, while Ethiopian and women workers of other nationalities have their concentration in Service, Shop and Market Sales and Legislators, Senior Officials and Managers respectively.

However, Eritrean women workers have an edge over their counterpart in the occupation of Clerks and, Service, Shop and Market Sales. While Ethiopians have concentration in the category of Clerks; Service Shop and Market Sales, and also in the Plant and Machine Operators and Assemblers.

Women workers of other nationality and Ethiopian have more fluctuations in the distribution of their total by occupation; while Eritrean women workers have less fluctuation in their distribution. Ethiopian women workers have more concentration in the Service, Shop and Market Sales than what Eritrean women workers have in the Elementary Occupations. Thus Eritrean women workers have better distribution over various occupations than the Ethiopians or other women workers.

7.6 Women Workers by Occupation and Educational Level

Education, in principle, has a direct bearing on the choice of occupation. It is assumed that employment in a particular occupation depends mainly upon the level of education, though there has been controversy and debate about the relevance of education to the world of work. Interesting facts and inferences may be expected from the analysis of occupational distribution of women workers in Eritrea.

Illiterate and primary educated women workers have concentration in the Elementary Occupations, while secondary educated have their largest percentage in the occupational category of Clerk. Around 90 per cent of certificate holders are Technicians and Associate Professionals. But diploma holders have their largest percentage in the category of Professionals followed by Clerks. University drop out are largely absorbed as Clerks followed by Professionals. More than two-fifth degree holders, one- half Masters and

TABLE 7.5: Women Workers by Occupation and Nationality

Occupation	Eritrean women workers	Per cent	Ethiopian women workers	Per cent	Other women workers	Per cent
Legislators, Sr. Officials Managers	996	7.6	74	3.1	6	40.0
Professionals	456	3.5	16	0.7	3	20.0
Technicians and Asso. Professionals	472	3.6	10	0.4	1	6.7
Clerks	1,902	14.5	130	5.4	1	6.7
Service, Shop and Mkt. Sales	1,419	10.8	919	38.4	2	13.3
Skilled Agri. and Fishery workers	12	0.1	4	0.2	–	–
Craft and Related Trades	1,749	13.4	121	5.0	–	–
Plant-Machine Oper. and Assem.	1,828	14.0	431	18.0	–	–
Elementary Occupation	4,250	32.5	689	28.8	2	13.3
Total	13,084	100.0	2,394	100.0	15	100.0

100 per cent Ph.D. holders are in the Professional's category.

In the occupational category of Legislators etc, Professionals, Technicians and Associated Professionals, and Clerks it may be observed that the percentage distribution of women workers goes up with the level of education. On the contrary, percentage of women workers largely declines as the level of education goes up in the case of the Service, Shop and Market Sales workers, skilled Agricultural and Fishery workers; Plant-Machine Operators and Assemblers; and tke Elementary Occupations.

7.7 Sum-up

Occupational distribution of women workers may be summed-up as:

- Occupational sex segregation in Eritrea has been moderate since Dissimilarity Index, D, comes to 50 per cent. Relatively speaking Craft and Related Trades and Elementary Occupations show larger segregation than other occupations.
- Women have a higher than average share in permanent employment, but lower in temporary jobs. Moreover, women Workers have less percentage as Professionals, Technicians and Associate Professionals in the permanent employment and Legislators, Senior Officials and Managers in addition to two aforementioned occupations in the category of temporary employment;
- Distribution of women workers by job-relations and occupation shows largest percentage of salaried workers in the Elementary Occupations; while employers' category of women has concentration in the Legislators, Senior Officials and Managers' category. Family women workers are mainly in the category of the Service, Shop and Market Sales followed by Legislators, Senior Officials and Managers. Lastly, apprentice women workers have their largest percentage in the Craft and Related Trades, closely followed by Legislators, Senior Officials and Managers. Thus distribution of women workers by job-relations differ from occupation to occupation.

TABLE 7.6: Women Workers by Occupation and Educational Level

Occupation	Illi.	Prim.	Sec.	Certi.	Dip.	Uni.	Deg. Inc.	Mas.	Ph.D.	Total
A. Legislators, Sr. Officials and Managers	294 (6.2)	295 (6.5)	373 (6.7)	–	32 (11.1)	41 (22.5)	39 (30.0)	2 (28.6)	–	1,076
B. Professionals	10 (0.2)	32 (0.7)	220 (3.9)	–	102 (35.2)	52 (28.6)	53 (40.8)	4 (57.1)	2 (100.0)	475
C. Technicians and Asso. Professionals	31 (0.7)	55 (1.2)	357 (6.4)	8 88.9	13 (4.5)	14 (7.7)	4 (3.1)	1 (14.3)	–	483
D. Clerks	62 (1.3)	172 (3.8)	1,631 (29.1)	1 (11.1)	80 (27.7)	58 (31.9)	29 (22.3)	–	–	2,033
E. Service, Shop and Market Sales	623 (13.1)	830 (18.4)	877 (15.7)	–	2 (0.7)	5 (2.7)	3 (2.3)	–	–	2,340
F. Skilled Agri. and Fishery Workers	8 (0.2)	1 (0.02)	7 (0.1)	–	–	–	–	–	–	16
G. Craft and Related Trades	597 (12.5)	528 (11.7)	695 (12.4)	–	45 (15.6)	5 (2.7)	–	–	–	1,870
H. Plant-Machine Oper. and Assem.	1,130 (23.7)	737 (16.3)	374 (6.7)	–	12 (4.2)	4 (2.2)	2 (1.5)	–	–	2,259
I. Elementary Occupations	2,004 (42.1)	1,868 (41.3)	1,063 (19.0)	–	3 (1.0)	3 (1.7)	–	–	–	4,941
Total	4,759 (100.0)	4,518 (100.0)	5,597 (100.0)	9 (100.0)	289 (100.0)	182 (100.0)	130 (100.0)	7 (100.0)	2 (100.0)	15,493

Note: Figure in parenteses show per cent of col. total.

- Women workers by age-distribution show that women in the age range of 19 to 29 are largely concentrated in the Service, Shop and Market Sales; Elementary Occupations; Technicians and Associate Professionals; Clerks; Skilled Agri. and Fishery Works; Craft and Related Trades. While women workers in the age range of 30 to 59 fall in the rest of occupation. Women workers of 60 and above are largely either in Legislators, Senior Officials and Managers occupational category or in the Elementary Occupations.
- Nationality-wise distribution of women workers shows that Eritrean women dominate in the Elementary Occupations, while Ethiopians have largest percentage of their total in the Service, Shop and Market Sales.
- Distribution of women workers by occupation and educational level shows largest percentage of illiterates and primary educated in the Elementary Occupation; secondary educated in the Clerical category; graduate, post-graduate (Masters) and Ph.Ds. in the occupational category of Professionals.

However, the striking feature with respect to occupational distribution of women workers has been occupational sex segregation to the extent of 0.5 which is compatible even with developed countries.

Note

$$D = \tfrac{1}{2} \sum_{1=1}^{n} \left| (Wi/W) - (Mi/M) \right| \times 100$$

Where Wi = Women in occupation i

W = Total women

Mi = Men in occupation i

M = Total Men

n = No. of occupations

"D varies from 0 to 100, with 0 representing a perfectly even distribution and 100 representing perfect segregation."

8

Wage Structure

8.0 Introduction

Inequality in wages for women vis-a-vis men workers has been in practice since a long time. It has infact, been the single most important parameter to measure the extent of gender inequality at work and many studies have their focus on this particular aspect (Jacobs, 1995).

Eritrea has a proportion of 34 per cent of women in total employment in its establishments. Hence, it is pertinent to study wage levels of women workers and compare with that of male workers to draw inferences regarding the prevalence of gender-wage inequality at work.

8.1 Women Workers By Wage-Level

Wage payments have been classified into four viz. low-income group, middle income group, upper-middle income group, and upper income group, keeping in view the socioeconomic structure of the society. Low-income group covers monthly wages 0-700 Nakfa, middle income group 701-1,600, upper-middle income group 1,601 and 2,500 and upper income group payment in the range of 2501 and 3,100 and above. Distribution of women workers by wage levels has been given in Table 8.1.

Distribution of women workers by wage level is such that 88.6 per cent of total fall in the low-income group, 10.1 per cent in the middle income group, 1 per cent in the upper-middle and, 0.3 per

TABLE 8.1: Women Workers by Wage Levels

Wage level	No. of women workers	Per cent	Per cent of total	Per cent in the slab	Per cent of male workers	Per cent of male total
Low Income Gr.						
0-100	2,152	15.7	13.9	36.9	18.5	12.2
101-200	2,745	20.0	17.7	68.5	6.3	4.2
201-300	3,220	23.5	20.8	61.3	10.2	6.7
301-400	3,125	22.8	20.2	36.4	27.4	18.1
401-500	1,491	10.8	9.6	31.5	16.2	10.7
501-600	581	4.2	3.8	19.1	12.3	8.1
601-700	415	3.0	2.7	18.6	9.1	6.0
Sub-Total	13,729	100.0	88.7	40.7	100.0	66.1
Middle Income Gr.						
701-1,000	821	52.6	5.3	14.5	56.1	16.0
1,001-1,300	477	30.5	3.1	15.5	30.3	8.6
1,301-1,600	264	16.9	1.7	18.4	13.6	3.9
Sub-Total	1562	100.0	10.1	15.4	100.0	28.5
Middle Income Gr.						
1,601-1,900	81	49.7	0.5	12.2	48.6	1.9
1,901-2,200	54	33.1	0.3	11.8	33.9	1.3
2,201-2,500	28	17.2	0.2	11.8	17.5	0.7
Sub-Total	163	100.0	1.0	35.8	100.0	4.0
Upper Income Gr.						
2,501-2,800	13	33.3	0.08	14.1	18.3	0.2
2,801-3,100	9	23.1	0.06	8.0	23.9	0.3
3,101 and >	17	43.6	0.11	6.4	57.8	0.8
Sub-Total	39	100.0	0.25	8.3	100.0	1.4
Total	15,493	100.0	100.0	33.9	100.0	66.1

cent in the upper income group. On the contrary, distribution for male workers has been 66.1 per cent, 28.5 per cent, 4 per cent and 1.4 per cent for low, middle, upper-middle and upper income groups respectively. It clearly shows that larger percentage of women workers fall in the low income group, while still a larger (than that of women) percentage of male workers fall in higher income groups.

Women workers have their concentration in 201-300 Nakfa slab of low-income group, 701-1,000 Nakfa slab of middle income group, 1,601-1,900 and, 3,101 and above slabs of upper-middle and upper income groups. While male workers show it for 301-400, 701-1,000, 1,601-1,900 and 3101 and above income slabs, showing relatively better position of male workers in the low-income group. Moreover, male workers have larger percentage than women workers for every higher slab of each income group.

Disparity between wages of women and men workers is also shown by the average wage in each, except middle, income group. Wormen workers have averages of 267.9, 1,042.4, 1,952.4 and 2,980.8 Nakfa for low, middle, upper middle and upper income groups. While these are 340.05, 1,022.6, and 1,956.9 and 3,068.3 Nakfa respectively for male workers. Therefore, women have less average wage in low, upper-middle and upper income groups as compared with the wages of male workers, The disparity widens between average wage of women and men worker when it is calculated in their respective total wage bills. It comes to 370.60 Nakfa for women workers and 637.60 Nakfa for male workers. On the whole, women workers receive far less than male workers from the total wage bill. Women workers get even less than the average total wage, which comes to 547.05 Nakfa, while male workers get over and above the average of total wages, as shown below.

Hence, gender wage inequality prevails in the establishments in Eritrea, confirming the general pattern of wage inequality by sex in developing countries.

8.2 Women Workers by Job-Nature and Wage Level

The preceding section, i.e. 7.1 makes it safe to presume that wage inequality would be there whether permanent or temporary employment of women. It is now to be seen which of these has larger inequality in wage level. Consider Table 8.2 to draw inferences in this regard.

Women workers in permanent employment have as high as 85 per cent of their total in low-income group, 13.2 per cent in middle, 1.4 per cent and 0.4 per cent in upper-middle and upper income groups respectively. While these figures are more skewed for temporary women workers. Moreover, there are no temporary women workers in the upper income group.

TABLE 8.2: Women Workers by Job-Nature and Wage Level

Wage level	Permanent women workers				Temporary women workers			
	No.	Per cent	Per cent of income group	Per cent of total workers	No.	Per cent	Per cent of income group	Per cent of total workers
Low Income Gr.								
0-100	1,737	16.1	18.9	11.2	415	8.8	9.1	2.7
101-200	1,279	11.9	13.9	8.3	1,466	31.2	32.2	9.5
201-300	2,308	21.4	25.2	14.9	912	19.4	20.0	5.9
301-400	2,036	18.9	22.2	13.1	1,089	23.2	23.9	7.0
401-500	1,016	9.4	11.0	6.6	475	10.1	10.4	3.1
501-600	449	4.2	4.9	2.9	132	2.8	2.9	0.9
601-700	347	3.2	3.8	2.2	68	1.4	1.5	0.4
Sub-Total	9,172	85.0	100.0	59.2	4,557	96.9	100.0	29.4
Middle Income Gr.								
701-1,000	737	6.8	51.7	4.8	84	1.8	61.3	0.5
1,001-1,300	446	4.1	31.3	2.9	31	0.7	226	0.2
1,301-1,600	242	2.2	17.0	1.6	22	0.5	16.1	0.1
Sub-Total	1,425	13.2	100.0	9.2	137	2.9,	100.0	0.9

Upper Middle Income Gr.								
1,601-1,900	80	0.7	51.6	0.5	1	0.02	12.5	0.006
1,901-2,200	52	0.5	33.5	0.3	2	0.04	25.0	0.013
2,201-2,500	23	0.2	14.8	0.1	5	0.11	62.5	0.032
Sub-Total	155	1.4	100.0	10	8	0.17	100.0	0.05
Upper Income Gr.								
2,501-2,800	13	0.12	33.3	0.08	–	–	–	–
2,801-3,100	9	0.08	23.1	0.06	–	–	–	–
3,101 and >	17	0.16	43.6	0.11	–	–	–	–
Sub-Total	39	0.4	100.0	0.25	–	–	–	
Total	10,791	100.0	69.7	69.7	4,702	100.0	–	30.3

Average income of permanent women workers has been more than temporary workers in the low, middle and upper income groups.

Women workers in permanent employment, are better placed than temporary women workers. Hence, wage disparity is there not only between women and men workers but between permanent and temporary women workers as well.

It is evident that women workers in the permanent employment have higher average than their counterpart in the middle income group only. Whereas, temporary women workers show higher average wages than male workers in the middle and upper-middle incomc groups. In the rest of income groups, male workers have higher average earnings than women workers. Moreover, there are no temporary women workers in the upper income group. Wage inequality in both the categories of employment is visible for women workers vis-a-vis male workers.

8.3 Women Workers by Job-Relations and Wage Level

Intra-group variations in wage level indicate wage inequality by job-relations. It is to be estimated how much wage inequality exists between salaried women workers, employers, family workers and apprentices. Table 8.3 shows distribution of women workers in various categories and their respective wage levels.

Salaried women workers have 87.5 per cent while employers, family workers and apprentice categories show 98.1 per cent, 99.3 per cent and 97.7 per cent of their respective total in the low income group. In terrns of percentage distribution by wage level, salaried women workers have significant difference while the latter three categories are very close to each other.

However, wage inequality between these four categories may be judged from their respective average wages. Average for salaried women workers comes to 294.6 Nakfa per month while it is 59.5, 57.0 and 73.8 Nakfa only for employers, family workers and apprentices in the low income group.

In the middle income group, averages come to 1040.1, 892.9, 1000 and 850 Nakfa for salaried workers, employers, family workers and apprentices respectively.

TABLE 8.3: Women Workers by Job-Relations and Wage Level

Wage levels	Salaried	Per cent	Employer	Per cent	Family workers	Per cent	Apprentice	Per cent
Low Income Gr.								
0-100	671	4.8	781	91.8	666	95.8	34	79.1
101-200	2,699	19.4	25	2.9	15	1.4	6	14.0
201-300	3,207	23.1	9	1.1	2	9.3	2	4.7
301-400	3,109	22.4	3	1.5	3	0.4	–	–
401-500	1,486	10.7	4	0.5	1	0.1	–	–
501-600	577	4.1	2	0.2	2	0.3	–	–
601-700	413	3.0	1	0.1	1	0.1	–	–
Sub-Total	12,162	87.5	835	98.1	690	99.3	42	97.7
Middle Income Gr.								
701-1,000	813	5.8	6	0.7	1	0.1	1	2.3
1,001-1,300	475	3.4	1	0.1	1	0.1	–	–
1,301-1,600	260	1.9	–	–	–	–	–	–
Sub-Total	1,552	11.2	7	0.8	2	0.3	1	2.3
Upper-Middle Income Gr.								
1,601-1,900	81	0.6	–	–	–	–	–	–
1,901-2,200	50	0.4	2	0.2	2	0.3	–	–
2,201-2500	26	0.2	2	0.2	–	–	–	–
Sub-Total	157	1.1	4	0.5	2	0.3	–	–

(*Contd.*)

Wage levels	Salaried	Per cent	Employer	Per cent	Family workers	Per cent	Apprentice	Per cent
Upper Income Gr.								
2,501-2,800	13	0.09	–	–	–	–	–	–
2,801-3,100	6	0.04	3	0.4	–	–	–	–
3,101 and >	14	0.10	5	0.6	1	0.1	–	–
Sub-Total	33	0.2	5	0.6	1	0.1	–	–
Total	13,904	100.0	851	100.0	695	100.0	43	100.0

Similarly, averages in the upper-middle income group for these categories have been 1944.9, 2200 and 2050 Nakfa. There is no apprentice in the upper-middle and upper income groups.

Lastly, upper income group shows average for salaried, employers and family women workers as 2959.1, 3070 and 3250 Nakfa per month.

Salaried women workers have higher average in the low and middle income groups, employer women workers in the upper-middle income group, while family women workers show higher average in the upper income group. Therefore, each category of women workers dominates in an income group though different from each other.

Comparing with the average wages of male workers, women workers in all the categories receive less in the low income group, while a totally inverse situation has been noticed in the middle income group. Male workers receive higher wages in the salaried class of upper-middle income group but less for employers and family workers' categories. In the upper income group average wages for male workers are higher than that of female workers.

Therefore, wage inequality exists not only between various categories of women workers but also between male and women workers in various categories. Gender inequality at work, in terms of wage, is in prevalence in the establishments and, that too, not in favour of women workers.

8.4 Women Workers by Age and Wage Level

Wage levels have a relation with the age of workers since the latter implies experience and skill acquisition. It is hypothesized that workers senior in age and possessing skills and or experience may be drawing higher wages than young entrants in the labour market. Table 8.4 shows distribution of women workers by age and wage levels. Distribution of women workers has been such that less than or equal to 19 year age have 99.3 per cent of their group total in the low income group and only 0.7 per cent in the middle income group. The percentage of group total falls till the age group of 35-39 years and then rises till 60≥ age group while middle-upper, middle and upper income groups show concentration of

TABLE 8.4: Distribution of Female Workers by Age and Wage Level

Wage levels	No. of female workers by age groups									
	≤ 19	20-24	25-29	30-34	35-39	40-44	45-49	50-54	55-59	60 ≥
Low Income Gr.										
0-100	465	299	252	216	226	217	179	115	79	104
101-200	832	674	429	173	208	161	125	69	34	40
201-300	297	450	615	504	460	405	277	130	56	26
301-400	328	379	533	326	337	308	431	306	69	18
401-500	34	188	316	213	212	175	173	132	38	10
501-600	11	73	148	89	75	81	66	28	7	3
601-700	6	44	133	68	57	51	30	17	8	1
Sub-Total	1,973	2,107	2,426	1,589	1,575	1,488	1,281	797	291	202
	(99.3)	(94.4)	(87.3)	(81.0)	(80.0)	(84.0)	(91.9)	(90.5)	(94.2)	(95.7)
Middle Income Gr.										
701-1,000	5	86	217	186	151	96	48	22	3	7
1,001-1,300	6	19	85	107	99	77	33	40	10	1
1,301-1,600	2	18	32	50	90	47	11	13	1	–
Sub-Total	13	123	334	343	340	220	92	75	14	8
	(0.7)	(5.5)	(17.5)	(17.5)	(17.3)	(12.5)	(6.6)	(8.5)	(4 5)	(3.8)
Upper-Middle Income Gr.										
1,601-1,900	–	–	6	12	28	28	4	2	1	–
1,901-2,200	–	1	6	5	14	20	3	4	1	–

2,201-2,500	–	–	5	5	4	6	6	1	–	–
Sub-Total	–	1	17	22	46	54	13	7	2	–
		(0.05)	(0.6)	(1.1)	(2.6)	(3.0)	(0.9)	(0.3)	(0.6)	
Upper Income Gr.										
2,501-2,800	–									
2,801-3,100	–									
3,101 and >	–									
Sub-Total		1	2	7	8	9	8	2	2	1
		(0.05)	(0.1)	(0.4)	(0.5)	(0.8)	(0.2)	(0.6)	(0.5)	
Total	1,986	2,232	2,779	1,961	1,969	1,771	1,394	881	309	211
	12.8	14.4	17.9	12.7	12.7	11.4	9.0	5.7	2.0	1.4

Note: Figures in parentheses show per cent of column total.

women workers in the age-range of 25-40, 30-45 and 30-50 years respectively. It indicates higher wages for workers with some seniority of age.

Women workers of 19-29 age range show an increasing average in the low and upper income groups while falling averages for middle and upper-middle income groups. Age range 30-39 shows declining average for low and upper middle income groups and rising averages for women workers falling in the middle and upper income groups. Similarly, 40-49 age range shows increasing averages for low and upper middle income groups and declining for the middle and upper income groups. Women workers in the age range of 50-59 show decreasing averages for low, middle and upper-middle income groups but increasing for the upper income group. Lastly, age range 60≥ has the lowest average for women workers in every income group.

Moreover, highest average in the low, middle, upper-middle and upper income groups pertain to women workers in the age groups of 50-54, again 50-54, 45-49 and 55-59 years respectively indicating a positive relation in the seniority of age and average wage.

8.5 Women Workers by Nationality and Wage Level

Women workers by nationality have been categorized into three viz. Eritrean, Ethiopian and others. Their distribution by wage levels has been given below.

The average income of Eritrean women worker comes to 287.4 Nakfa in the low income group, higher than that of Ethiopian, i.e. 175.1 and others 170.0 Nakfa per month. The same pattern has been observed for the middle income group where average wages for Eritrean, Ethiopian and other women workers have been 1,044.6, 940 and 850 Nakfa respectively.

In the upper-middle income, Ethiopian women workers have higher average than Eritreans since the average wages are 2,250, 2,200 and 1,943.7 for Ethiopian, others and Eritrean women workers respectively. The same pattern has been for upper income group where averages for Eritrean, Ethiopian and others have been 2,966.2, 3,250, 3,250 respectively.

TABLE 8.5: Women Workers by Nationality and Wages

Wage level	Eritrean	Per cent	Ethiopian	Per cent	Others	Per cent
Low Income Gr.						
0-100	1,607	14.2	538	22.7	7	70.0
101-200	1,549	13.6	1,196	50.5	–	–
201-300	2,923	25.8	297	12.5	–	–
301-400	2,902	25.7	223	9.3	2	20.0
401-500	1,406	12.4	85	3.6	–	–
501-600	555	4.9	26	1.1	–	–
601-700	407	3.6	7	0.3	1	10.0
Sub-Total	11,349	100.0	2,370	100.0	10	100.0
	(86.7)		(99.0)		(66.7)	
Middle Income Gr.						
701-1,000	803	52.1	16	80	2	100.0
1,001-1,300	475	30.8	2	10	–	–
1,301-1,600	262	17.1	2	10	–	–
Sub-Total	1,540	100.0	20	100.0	2	100.0
	(11.8)		(0.8)		(33.3)	
Upper-Middle Income Gr.						
1,601-1,900	81	51.3	–	–	–	–
1,901-2,200	52	32.9	1	33.4	1	50.0
2,201-2,500	25	15.8	2	66.6	1	50.0
Sub-Total	158	100.0	3	100.0	2	100.0
	(1.2)		(0.13)		(13.3)	
Upper Income Gr.						
2,501-2,800	13	351	–	–	–	–
2,801-3,100	9	243	–	–	–	–
3,101 and >	13	40.5	1	100.0	1	100.0
Sub-Total	37	100.0	1	100.0	1	100.0
	(0.3)		(0.04)		(6.7)	
Total	13,084	84.5	2,394	15.4	15	0.1

However average wage for Eritrean, in their total wage bill comes to 404.1 Nakfa,, 185.4 for Ethiopians and 736.7 for women of other nationality. Whatever criteria be chosen to find out the average wages, there is wide disparity between averages for women workers of these nationalities.

Comparing wage levels by gender and nationality, Eritrean males have higher wage average than Eritrean women workers in all, except middle income, groups. An inverse situation exists for Ethiopians where women workers have higher wage average in all but low income group. While women workers of other nationality show higher than male's average wage in the upper-middle and upper income groups.

Hence these are Eritrean women workers who are relatively worst off as compared with women workers of either Ethiopia or other nationality vis-a-vis their counterparts in terms of average wage.

Similarly, comparing the average wages of male and women workers by nationality, Eritrean women get average wage 61.1 per cent of male worker, Ethiopian 44.8 per cent and other 66.9 per cent of male workers of respective nationality. Therefore, women workers of other nationality are better-off than Eritrean and Ethiopian women workers. However, Eritrean women workers are better off than Ethiopian female workers. Wage inequality in terms of gender exists in wage earnings of workers of different nationality.

8.6 Women Workers by Educational and Wage Level

It is argued that education has little relevance to the world of work. Therefore no direct relation may be expected between the levels of education and wages. However data analysis is supposed to accept or reject the hypothesis stated above. Following table shows distribution of women workers by education and wages levels.

Analysis by wage levels presents a contradictory picture. Illiterates, for example, have higher average of wage i.e. 261.2 Nakfa in the low income group than school-leavers and even first degree holders (181.8 Nakfa). It is equally surprising that illiterate women workers are not only there in the upper income group but also their average wage, i.e. 3250 Nakfa has been higher than that of school-leavers and even greater than that of first degree holder's average wage in the upper income group as well. Hence data collected needs some careful scrutiny and review of classification.

However, distribution of women workers by educational and wage levels may be seen from Table 8.6.

Average analysis, based on Table 8.6 makes it easy to understand the relative position of women workers, in terms of wages, by their education level.

TABLE 8.6: Distribution of Female Workers by the Levels of Wage and Education

Wage levels	No. of female by educational level								
	Illi.	Prim.	Sec.	Cert.	Dip.	Univ. income	First degree	Master	Ph.D.
I. Low Income Gr.									
0-100	659	745	705	1	10	19	14	–	–
101-200	1,023	948	770	–	1	2	1	–	–
201-300	1,068	1,098	1,043	–	3	6	2	–	–
301-400	1,301	981	836	–	3	3	1	–	–
401-500	478	426	577	1	1	8	1	–	–
501-600	129	122	310	2	14	4	1	–	–
601-700	56	66	278	2	5	6	2	–	–
Sub-Total	4,714	4,386	4,519	6	37	48	22	–	–
	(99.0)	(97.1)	(80.7)	(14.0)	(12.8)	(26.4)	(16.9)		
II. Middle Income Gr.									
701-1,000	40	63	598	13	65	45	6	–	1
1,001-1,300	2	37	284	19	91	42	18	1	–
1,300-1,600	2	25	119	4	60	23	33	1	–
Sub-Total	44	125	1,001	36	216	110	57	2	1
	(0.9)	(2.8)	(17.9)	(83.7)	(74.7)	(60.4)	(43.8)	(28.6)	(50.0)
III. Upper Middle Income Gr.									
1,601-1,900	–	3	44	–	12	12	9	1	–
1,901-2,200	–	1	21	–	13	4	14	–	1

(Contd.)

Wage levels	No. of female by educational level								
	Illi.	Prim.	Sec.	Cert.	Dip.	Univ. income	First degree	Master	Ph.D.
2,201-2,500	–	3	7	–	1	3	13	1	–
Sub-Total	–	7	72	–	26	19	36	2	1
		(0.2)	(1.3.)		(9.0)	(10.4)	(27.7)	(28.6)	(50.0)
IV. Upper Income Gr.									
2,501-2,800	–	–	–	–	4	2	7	–	–
2,801-3,100	–	–	2	–	2	1	3	1	–
3,100 and >	1	–	3	1	4	2	5	2	–
Sub-Total	1	–	5	1	10	5	15	3	–
	(0.1)		(0.1)	(2.3)	(3.5)	(2.7)	(11.5)	(42.8)	
Total	4,759	4,518	5,597	43	289	182	130	7	2
Per cent of total	(30.6)	(29.1)	(36.0)	(0.3)	(1.9)	(1.2)	(0.8)	(0.05)	(0.01)

Women workers falling in the low income group do not show any consistency in averages in terms of educational level. But middle and upper-middle income groups depict lower average wage for illiterates and higher averages for educated women workers. However, upper income group indicates inverse relation between average wage and educational level since there are high average for lower educational level and its vice-versa. It may be true for establishments which have employed women workers with education due to lack of sufficient manpower and not specifically for their certificate and degree. This aspect needs some more research in the next round of survey.

However, average wages computed from total wage bill by educational levels make it clear that graduate get higher average wage (151 Nfa) than Secondary (442.1 Nfa), Primary (275.7) educated and illiterate women workers (267.6). The aggregate analysis clears distortions at desegregated level i.e. different wage levels. The final picture based on average total wages by educational levels establish a positive relationship between educational and wage levels

Since there is a positive and direct relationship between the average wage of women workers and their educational level, the hypothesis that education has little relevance to the world of work (and hence wages), may be refuted very strongly. It also indicates a rational wage-structure in prevalence in Eritrea.

8.7 Wage Level by Industrial Activity

Women workers classified by industrial activity need to be analyzed in terms of wage level in order to know their relative position in various industrial activities. Table 8.7 shows distribution of women workers by industrial activity and wage levels.

Out of total women workers, 88.6 per cent fall in the low income, 10.1 per cent in the middle income, 1 per cent in the upper-middle and 0.3 per cent in the upper income group.

However, percentage distribution of wornen workers by industrial sector, in terms of wages, shows that the General Service; Agriculture, Hunting and Forestry; Construction; Manufacturing sectors have over 90 per cent of their total women workers in the low income group. Finance and Real Estate Renting; and Transport,

TABLE 8.7: Women Workers by Wages and Industrial Activity

Wage level	Industrial activity										
	A	B	C	D	E	F	G	H	I	J	K
0-100	6	–	398	–	12	4	373	1	–	1,335	23
101-200	7	–	437	4	6	8	406	7	12	1,838	20
201-300	28	–	2,156	–	4	100	250	54	5	587	36
301-400	259	–	1,298	10	47	1,002	85	183	44	169	28
401-500	5	3	901	2	97	220	53	66	11	106	27
501-600	9	–	302	–	12	82	47	62	18	37	12
601-700	1	–	150	6	21	60	44	78	16	27	12
Sub-Total	315	3	5,642	22	199	1,476	1,258	451	106	4,099	158
	(97.5)		(92.6)	(73.3)	(62.8)	(93.1)	(87.4)	(48.3)	(30.3)	(98.2)	(6.2)
Middle Income Gr.											
701-1,000	5	–	221	1	52	74	86	182	119	39	42
1,001-1,300	2	–	112	1	33	13	38	179	63	16	20
1,301-1,600	1	–	69	1	26	8	23	72	44	10	10
Sub-Total	8	–	402	3	111	95	147	433	226	65	72
	(2.5)		(6.6)	(10.0)	(35.0)	(6.0)	(10.2)	(46.4)	(64.6)	(1.5)	(29.3)
Upper Middle Income Gr.											
1,601-1,900	–	–	15	–	2	4	17	31	6	1	5
1,901-2,200	–	–	16	–	1	2	5	12	8	6	4
2,201-2,500	–	–	9	–	3	3	5	4	2	–	2
Sub-Total	–	–	40	–	6	9	27	47	16	7	11
			(0.7)		(1.9)	(0.6)	(1.9)	(5.1)	(4.6)	(0.2)	(4.5)

(Contd.)

Wage level	Industrial activity										
	A	B	C	D	E	F	G	H	I	J	K
Upper Income Gr.											
2,501-2,800	–	–	4	3	1	1	1	–	1	1	1
2,801-3,100	–	–	2	–	–	1	3	–	1	–	2
3,100 and >	–	–	1	2	–	3	4	2	–	3	2
Sub-Total	–	–	7	5	1	5	8	2	2	4	5
			(0.1)	(16.7)	(0.3)	(0.3)	(0.5)	(0.2)	(0.5)	(0.1)	(2.0)
Total	323	3	6,091	30	317	1,585	1,440	933	350	4,175	246
	(100.0)		(100.0)	(100.0)	(100.0)	(100.0)	(100.0)	(100.0)	(100.0)	(100.0)	(100.0)

Storage and Communication and, to some extent, Professional Service sectors have significant percentage of their total women workers in the middle income group. While Mining and Quarrying sector shows a considerable proportion of its total women workers in the upper income group.

Average wages of women workers by wage level and industrial activity have been shown below. Disparity in average wages is visible not only intra-group but inter-group as well. The highest average wage of women workers in the low income category has been 428.3 Nakfa in the Transport, Storage and Communication sector while lowest, in the same category, is the General Service sector (156.7 Nakfa)

Similarly, middle income category of women workers shows highest and lowest average wage for the Mining and Quarrying (1150 Nfa) and, Construction (911.6 Nfa). These are highest and lowest for the Electricity, Gas and Water Supply sector (2100 Nfa) and Transport, Storage and Communication sector (1916 Nfa) in the upper middle income group of women workers.

Lastly, upper income group of women workers shows highest (3250 Nfa) and lowest averages (2650 Nfa) for the Transport, Storage and Communication, and Electricity, Gas and Water Supply sectors. Hence wide disparity are there in the average wage of women workers employed in various industrial activities.

Moreover, wage inequality is obvious from the averages of women workers' income in the low, middle, upper-middle and upper income groups, i.e. 267.9 1093, 963.5 and 2980.8 Nakfa respectively. It shows significant variations in the average wages of women workers.

Average of total wage bill of women workers comes to 376.4 Nakfa which may be used as a yardstick to find out the extent of disparity in average wages. The inequality increases by the level of wages of women workers.

Another way of showing wage inequality by industrial activity is taking the average wage of women workers in each sector. The average wage of women workers differs from sector to sector.

Finance and Real Estate Renting has the highest average, i.e. 909.4 Nfa. While Construction sector shows it as meager as 112.9 Nfa only. Therefore, wage inequality is pronounced in terms of average wage of women workers by industrial activity in Eritrea.

8.8 Wage and Occupational Structure of Women Workers

Women workers by occupation have been classified into nine major categories as per the ISCO-88 classification. Their distribution by wage levels in these occupations has been given in Table 8.8.

Average wages in low, middle, upper-middle and upper income groups of women workers vary between 98.6 and 425.2 Nakfa, between 923.5 and 1112.5 Nakfa, 1850 and 2087 Nakfa and, between 1950 and 2996.2 Nakfa respectively. Therefore, wage inequality does exists not only with in a group but also between various income groups of women workers.

The highest average has been found in the case of Professionals and the lowest for women workers in the occupation of the Service, Shop and Market Sales.

However, the average total wage comes to 370.2 Nakfa for women workers in all the occupations. Therefore, women workers in four occupations namely. Professionals, Technicians and Associate professionals, Clerks and, Craft and Related Trades get more than total average. Similarly, women workers in the occupational categories of Legislators, Senior Officials and Managers; Service, Shop and Market sales; Skilled Agricultural and Fishers workers; Plant- Machine Operator and Assemblers; and Elementary Occupations get average wages less than the total average wage.

8.9 Sum-up

Summary of the present chapter may be given as follows:

- Women workers, not legally but conventionally receive less wages as compared with their counterparts.
- The ratio of women workers falling in the low income category has been higher than that of men workers. Moreover, women workers have a lower ratio than their counterpart in the middle, upper-middle and upper income (wage) groups.
- Wage-inequality in the case of women workers has been more

TABLE 8.8: Women Workers by Occupation and Wage Level

Wage level	Industrial occupations								
	A	B	C	D	E	F	G	H	I
Low Income Gr.									
0-100	789	21	20	232	620	0	67	59	344
101-200	17	13	10	173	997	2	114	286	1,133
201-300	15	24	52	190	298	4	424	1,055	1,158
301-400	46	23	31	165	225	5	354	614	1,662
401-500	35	41	30	197	98	3	510	94	483
501-600	13	24	67	136	30	2	158	69	82
601-700	10	26	56	147	32	0	83	32	29
Sub-Total	925	172	266	1,240	2,300	16	1,710	2,209	4,891
Middle Income Gr.									
701-1000	34	96	77	435	24	-	88	27	40
1001-1300	31	96	93	198	6	-	32	15	6
1301-1600	23	51	31	111	5	-	32	8	3
Sub-Total	88	243	201	744	35	-	152	50	49
Upper Middle Income Gr.									
1601-1900	14	25	11	26	2	-	3	-	-
1901-2200	24	14	4	10	1	-	1	-	
2201-2500									
Sub-Total	17	13	-	6	2	-	-	-	1
Total	1,076	475	483	2,033	2,340	16	1,870	2,259	4,941

Note: A—I stand for Legislators, Senior Officials and Managers; Professionals; Technicians and Asso. Professionals; Clerks; Service, Shop and Mkt. Sales; Skilled Agriculture and Fishery Workers; Craft and Related Trades; Plant-Machine Operators and Assemblers; Elementary Occupations in that order.

than that of men workers, in every wage category.

- Wage-parity does not exists between permanently and temporarily employed women workers. Again, there is a disparity between permanent and temporary women workers vis-a-vis men workers falling in these categories.
- Disparity in wage levels has been found between various employment categories of women workers viz. salaried, employers, family workers and apprentices. Women workers get less average wage in all the categories than men workers but in the low income group. While middle income group shows an inverse situation. However, gender inequality, in terms of wage, does exist and that too, not in favour of women workers.
- Age distribution of women workers shows wage disparity between various age-groups. It is against them in the age-range of 19 years onwards, and in favour for the age range of 45 to 59 years. It indicates that age seniority meaning thereby experience and skill does matter and are primarily responsible for wage differential of women workers by age.
- Average wage by nationality has been highest for the women workers of Other nationality followed by Eritrean and Ethiopian women in that order. And there is wide disparity between the average wages of women workers by nationality.

Comparing with men workers, Eritrean women get around 61 per cent of their menfolk Ethiopian around 45 per cent and women of other nationalities employed in Eritrea receive a better proportion, i.e around 67 per cent of their counterparts. So wage inequality exists intra-group as well as inter- group, i.e. among women workers of different nationalities and also between women and men workers.

- Disaggregated analysis of average wage by educational level presents an irrational wage- structure. However, average total wage by educational categories shows a positive and direct relationship between educational level and wage paid to women workers. Higher the level of education, higher the average wage (from illiteracy to first degree) negates the hypothesis that education has little relevance to the world of work. It is, at least, not true in the case of wage averages found in Eritrea and hence, a rational wage structure does exists.

- Average wage of women workers show disparity between various sectors. Wage inequalities are more in the low income group of women workers than higher income groups. However, inter-group wage inequalities in terms of average wage are pronounced and significant.
- There are three sectors namely, Construction, General Trading and General Service where average wages of women workers are low and less than average total wage. Other sectors have their average wages exceeding the average total wage for all industrial activities.
- Occupational wage-structure also shows wide-spread disparity in the average wages. Out of nine major occupations, five viz. Legislators, Senior Officials and Managers; Service, Shop and market sales workers; Skilled Agriculture and Fishery Workers; Plant-Machine Operators and Assemblers, and Elementary Occupations have low average wages and less than average total wage of women workers. Only four occupational categories of women workers receive higher average wages than the average total wage. Therefore, occupational disparity in terms of wages are common and significant.

However, wage-structure largely indicates overwhelming majority of women workers in the low income group and gender wage-inequality is prominent, that too, not in favour of women workers. The relative position of women workers in employment in general and in terms of wages in particular speak for gender based inequality and disparity, to be taken care of.

9

Conclusions and Recommendations

9.0 Introduction

Gender inequality at work has been a common problem, especially in developing countries. Eritrea has no legal sanctions but societal forces have created inequalities, particularly wage differential for working women in various occupations and industrial activities. Labour laws of the country, as a corrective measure, have been enforced since independence to remove all sorts of inequalities and discrimination based upon, inter-alia, gender or sex. These laws are also in conformity with the ILO conventions and recommendations regarding employment in general and equal remuneration for equal work (Convention 111,1960) and discrimination in employment and occupation (Convention 156, 1983) in particular.

9.1 Conclusions

Women workers in the establishments constitute one-third of the labour force. They are around 36 per cent of total in the permanent employment but only 30 per cent in temporary employment. Moreover their participation in various categories of employment such as salaried workers, employers and, family workers has been lopsided as majority falls in the wage-employment. Women workers in the category of employers have insignificant participation thus casting aspersion on their economic empowerment.

Age distribution of women workers indicates preference for relatively young workers in the age range of 19 to 29 years. Their participation, especially beyond the age of 45 years, has been less, while it is not a case for men workers since their distribution till the age of 30, and then 30 to 60 years is fairly distributed. The same may not be claimed in the case of women workers.

- Analysis of women workers by nationality reveals overwhelming proportion of Eritrean women, i.e. 84 per cent in total women workers while the share of Ethiopian women workers has been around 15 per cent of the total. However, participation rate of the latter in their total labour has been higher than that of the former. Eritrean women constitute 33 per cent in total Eritrean workers while the Ethiopian women enjoy a little over 40 per cent representation in their total workers.
- An inverse relation has been observed between the level of education and number of women workers, that is, higher the educational level, lower is the number of women workers. It means illiterate category has more women workers than the graduates. However school-leavers i.e. primary and especially secondary educated women workers have largest percentage in their total employment. It is in conformity with the total employment pattern in the country. However, distribution of women workers vis-a-vis men workers shows higher percentage of illiterates and relatively lower percentage of educated ones at every level of education. It may be taken as an indicator of women's less access to education in the country.
- Women workers by industrial activity are concentrated in the Manufacturing and General Service sectors. Infact, they out number men in the General Service sector being around 60 per cent of total workers. However, they have very low participation level in certain sectors, e.g., Mining and Quarrying; Electricity, Gas and Water Supply.
- Illiterate women workers have concentration in the Agricultural, Hunting and Forestry and, Manufacturing sectors, while their percentage in the Transport, Storage and Communication; Financial Intermediaries; and Professional Service has been the least.

- Eritrean women workers dominate in the Manufacturing sector but Ethiopians have their concentration in the General Service sector. It indicates complementarily rather than competition between Eritrean and Ethiopian women workers.
- Occupational sex segregation has been moderate since Dissimilarity Index. D, comes to 50 per cent. However, Craft and Related Trades and, Elementary Occupations relatively have more sex segregation than any other occupational category.
- The ratio of women workers has been less in the occupational categories of Professionals; Technicians and Associated Professionals; and Legislators, Senior Officials and Managers in the permanent and temporary employment.
- Distribution of women workers by occupation and job-relation shows largest percentage in the Elementary Occupations, while as employers they have concentration in the category of Legislators, Senior Officials and Managers. Family women workers are maximum in the Service, Shop and Market Sales. As apprentice, women workers are largely in the Craft and Related Trades. Hence. occupational distribution and concentration of women workers differ from occupation to occupation.
- Relatively young women workers, i.e., 19 to 29 are largely in the Service. Shop and Market Sales; Elementary Occupations; Technicians; Clerks and, Craft and Related Trades. On the other hand, women workers in the age range of 30 to 60 have concentration in the occupation of Legislators, Senior Officials and Managers. and Professionals.
- Eritrean women by occupation have their large percentage in the Elementary Occupations, while Ethiopians are largely engaged in the Service, Shop and Market Sales.
- Women workers by education show larger percentage of illiterates and primary educated in the Elementary Occupations, secondary educated in the Clerical cadre, white graduates, masters and doctorates in the occupational category of Professionals. There is, therefore, a strong relation between occupation and the level of education, i.e. a relevance between education and the world of work.
- Women workers receive less wages as compared to men folk.

It is around 61 per cent of men workers for Eritrean and only 45 per cent of men's wages for Ethiopian women workers. Thus there is gender wage inequality, that too, in every category of employment and wage level.

- Wage disparity has also been observed between women workers falling in different age groups/range. Senior women workers in the age range of 45 to 60 years get more as compared to women workers in the age range of 19 to 39 may be because of their experience and skill acquisition over the years.
- Average wages for women workers by their educational level indicate a direct relation, since higher average wage comes for women workers with higher level of education. But it also shows inequality in wages of women workers with different educational levels. Moreover, there is a disparity between wages of women workers in the same income and educational category but in different occupations.

Thus, there is a case for gender inequality at work, though of a moderate degree. There are certain industrial activities and also occupational categories where inequalities are prominent, particularly wage differential. It calls for corrective measures and following are the recommendations:

9.2 Recommendations

- Employment, particularly gender based policy, has to be evolved and implemented to maintain a balance between the number of men and women workers in the labour force;
- A minimum, but equal, wage policy be enunciated and enforced strictly regardless of sector, occupation and sex;
- In order to promote and ensure equal opportunity of employment to women, certain reservation at every level may be considered till some balance is achieved.
- The Ministry of Labour and Human Welfare should establish a women employment cell to be responsible for the promotion of not only employment of women but also for creating a conducive environment facilitating women's

employment. It may be entrusted with the responsibility of gender studies, education and training need assessment so as to improve their access to employment.

- Economic empowerment of women should be given special emphasis. There is need of promoting women enterpreneurship and encourage employer's status of women workers. It requires, inter-alia, special financial provisions and support to women workers. For example, women may be given loan at concessional rate and tax holidays be longer so that they have necessary resources and time to establish themselves.
- Since a number of women get no opportunity to work due to their family responsibilities, cottage industry culture may be developed and awareness among women be raised regarding earning while working at their homes. Government establishments e.g. residential school, university, para-military and defence hospitals etc. may have it mandatory to purchase at least certain specified percentage of their requirement from the cottage-industry sector. An agency, such as, cooperative may co-ordinate it.
- Workers' Organizations may also be involved to sensitize the issue of women's access to employment in the context of equal partner in the society.
- Every organization or association of workers should have women's cell to safeguard the interest of women in the employmenr and also to redress the problem or grievances of employed women workers. They should be given training in Unionism in order to learn and practice collective bargaining.
- Women workers in the rural and informal sectors be motivated to have their pressure groups so that they can refuse to submit to discriminatory practices.
- Employers' Organization should draw up training programmes for women, particularly in management.
- International Labour Standards be implemented and followed by the Employers' Organization, especially concerning women workers.
- Accepting a minimum percentage of female apprentices should be binding upon organizations/establishments and

employers' organization be held liable for it.

- International Institutions and Organization be approached to provide technical assistance regarding educational and training programmes of females.
- Gender studies should be promoted concerning employment and international organizations be asked for funding such projects. A periodical review of women's employment situation may be made a plan component and international agencies be approached to fund it.

However, a mix of these recommendations is required to be implemented to promote employment and economic empowerment of women.

9.3 Area of Further Research

The following area of further research may be suggested.

- Women Employment in the Informal Sector: Since every African economy including Eritrea has a large informal sector and women workers are sizeable in number in the informal sector, hence it should be given priority for further research.
- Women Workers in the context of Family Responsibility: Women have the onus of family and women workers are no exception. It affects their employment opportunities and promotion avenues. The subject should be investigated to alleviate the plight of women in general and, working women in particular.
- Discriminatory Attitudes and Practices in Wage-Income and Employment of Women.

The topic should be essentially probed to counteract harmful attitudes and practices for women's employment and also for employed women workers.

Bibliography

Boserup, E. (1970), Women's Role in Economic Developmen, New York, St. Martin's Press.

ECA (1971), Factors Affecting Education, Training and Work Opportunities for Girls and Women with in the Context of Development, Addis Ababa, ECA.

ILO (1983a), Changing Position of Women in Society, Geneva, ILO.

(1983b), "Status of Women: Gloomy Situation", in the ILO, *Social and Labour Bulletin*, 4, Dec.

Ahooja-Patel K. (1986), Another Development with Women, Geneva, ILO.

Selassie, Seyoun G. (1986), "Patterns of Women's Employment in Africa" in JASPA/ILO (ed.), *The Challenge of Employment and Basic Needs in Africa*, Nairobi, OUP, p. 96.

Castley, Robert J.W. (1986), "Crisis inVuman-Resource Planning in Sub-Saharan Africa" in JASPA (ed.), *The Challenge of Employment and Basic Needs in Africa*, Nairobi, OUP, p. 316.

Clair, R. and Berger, I. (1986), *Women and Class in Africa*, New York, Africana, p. 31.

Sen, G. and Grown, C. (1987), Development, Crises and Alternative Visions, New York, *Monthly Review Press*, p. 96.

Cornia, Giovanni A. Jolly, R. and Stewart F. (eds.) (1987), *Adjustment with a Human Face*, New York, OUP.

Mueller, Dixon, R. and Anker, R.E. (1988), Assessing Women's Economic Contributions to Development, Geneva, ILO.

ILO (1991), ILO Standards and Action for the Elimination of Discrimination and the Promotion of Equality of Opportunity in Employment. Geneva. International Labour Standards Department, ILO.

Moser, C. (1991), "Genders Planning in the Third World: Meeting Practical and Strategic Needs" in Grant, R. and Newland K.(eds.), *Gender and International Relations*, Buckingham, Open University Press, pp. 103-106.

Palmer, I. (1991), Gender and Population in the Adjustment of African Economies: Planning for Change, Geneva, ILO.

ILO (1994), "Changing Role of Women in the Economy: Employment and Social Issues", Papers of the Governing body, Geneva, ILO.

The Govt. of the State of Eritrea (1994), Macro-Policy, Asmara, Section 13.5 Gender Issues, sub-sections a to e, pp. 43-44.

ILO (1995), Women Workers An annotated bibliography 1983-94, Geneva, ILO, p. V.

Snyder, Margret C. Tadesse, Mary (1995), *African Women and Development*, Johannesberg, WUP, p. 9.

NSO (1997), *Eritrea: Demographic and Health Survey 1995*, Calverton (Maryland), NSO & Macro International Inc., p. 16.

MLHW (2001), Employment Situation in Eritrea, Deptt. of Labour and Research and HRD Div., Figure 3.13, p. 14 (Mimeo.).

Index